T0146931

Scarlet Grace

A Firm Foundation for the Weary Woman

Jessica Stewart

WESTBOW
P R E S S®
A DIVISION OF THOMAS NELSON
& ZONDERVAN

Copyright © 2023 Jessica Stewart.

All rights reserved. No part of this book may be used or reproduced by
any means, graphic, electronic, or mechanical, including photocopying,
recording, taping or by any information storage retrieval system
without the written permission of the author except in the case of
brief quotations embodied in critical articles and reviews.

This book is a work of non-fiction. Unless otherwise noted, the author
and the publisher make no explicit guarantees as to the accuracy of
the information contained in this book and in some cases, names of
people and places have been altered to protect their privacy.

WestBow Press books may be ordered through booksellers or by contacting:

WestBow Press
A Division of Thomas Nelson & Zondervan
1663 Liberty Drive
Bloomington, IN 47403
www.westbowpress.com
844-714-3454

Because of the dynamic nature of the Internet, any web addresses or
links contained in this book may have changed since publication and
may no longer be valid. The views expressed in this work are solely those
of the author and do not necessarily reflect the views of the publisher,
and the publisher hereby disclaims any responsibility for them.

Any people depicted in stock imagery provided by Getty Images are
models, and such images are being used for illustrative purposes only.
Certain stock imagery © Getty Images.

ISBN: 979-8-3850-0742-4 (sc)
ISBN: 979-8-3850-0743-1 (hc)
ISBN: 979-8-3850-0744-8 (e)

Library of Congress Control Number: 2023917743

Print information available on the last page.

WestBow Press rev. date: 12/14/2023

Scripture quotations marked AMP are taken from the Amplified® Bible, Copyright © 1954, 1958, 1962, 1964, 1965, 1987 by The Lockman Foundation. Used by permission.

Scripture quotations marked NIV are taken from the Holy Bible, New International Version®, NIV®. Copyright © 1973, 1978, 1984 by Biblica, Inc.™ Used by permission of Zondervan. All rights reserved worldwide.

Scripture quotations marked NLT are taken from the Holy Bible, New Living Translation, copyright © 1996, 2004, 2007 by Tyndale House Foundation. Used by permission of Tyndale House Publishers, Inc., Carol Stream, Illinois 60188. All rights reserved.

Scripture quotations marked ESV are from the ESV Bible® (The Holy Bible, English Standard Version®), copyright © 2001 by Crossway Bibles, a publishing ministry of Good News Publishers. Used by permission. All rights reserved.

Scripture quotations marked NKJV are taken from the New King James Version. Copyright © 1982 by Thomas Nelson, Inc. Used by permission. All rights reserved.

Scripture quotations marked NET are from the NET Bible® copyright ©1996-2016 by Biblical Studies Press, L.L.C. All rights reserved.

To Priscilla
You have walked beside me through many long and hard years. Your unwavering love and friendship have continually comforted and refreshed my soul.

To Colleen
Without you, this book never would have been written. I am profoundly grateful for you and your continuous support and encouragement over the years.

CONTENTS

PREFACE

The idea of writing is a seed the Lord planted in me long ago. Over the years, He has brought others along, quite unexpectedly, to water that seed, and He has provided the light needed for it to grow slowly but surely. However, it wasn't until the beginning of 2019 that this seed all of a sudden had a growth spurt and truly became something viable. I spent months in prayer seeking the Lord and His will regarding all of this with the expectation that He would make things clear. As the months went by, God began showing me that my desire to speak truth and life into the hearts and lives of women—words that give encouragement, hope, and healing to the hearts and minds of those who are broken and suffering—are actually gifts He's given me; spiritual gifts of mercy, encouragement, and compassion. I believe one of the ways He wants me to serve Him and His people, as well as to reach out to those who don't yet know Christ, is through writing.

For many years, I have desired and prayed for Jesus to continue His ministry through me; His ministry described in Isaiah 61:1–4:

> The Spirit of the Sovereign LORD is on me, because the LORD has anointed me to proclaim good news to the poor. He has sent me to bind up the brokenhearted, to proclaim freedom for the captives and release from darkness for the prisoners, to proclaim the year of the LORD's favor and the day of vengeance of our God, to comfort all who

mourn, and provide for those who grieve in Zion—
to bestow on them a crown of beauty instead of
ashes, the oil of joy instead of mourning, and a
garment of praise instead of a spirit of despair. They
will be called oaks of righteousness, a planting of
the LORD for the display of his splendor. They will
rebuild the ancient ruins and restore the places long
devastated; they will renew the ruined cities that
have been devastated for generations. (NIV)

This is what I long to do—to be a part of this process in the lives of
others in whatever way God sees fit.

More time spent in prayer and in His Word over the months revealed
that my first writing assignment was this right here: fifty-two
devotions, one for each week over the course of a year. My hope and
fervent prayer are that these weekly devotions will bless you, comfort
you, and encourage you. I hope that they will lift your head to your
great and precious Father and Savior, "the Father of compassion and
the God of all comfort, who comforts us in all our troubles, so that
we can comfort those in any trouble with the comfort we ourselves
receive from God" (2 Cor. 1:3 [NIV]).

ACKNOWLEDGEMENTS

To Rich- Your sacrificial love has provided the time and space needed to make this book possible. Thank you for believing in me wholeheartedly and reassuring me in times of doubt. I love you.

To the original group of women who received these weekly devotions- Thank you for being a part of this journey. Your heartfelt responses encouraged me and reaffirmed God's call to pick up my pen and write these 52 devotions. I am grateful to each of you for trusting me to speak to your hearts.

Most importantly, to our Great God and Savior- I thank You and praise You for Your immeasurable grace, incomparable love, and unyielding faithfulness; for the privilege of writing this book and for the plans and purposes You have for it. To Your name alone be the glory!

INTRODUCTION

Scarlet Grace is a devotional written to usher women into the presence of their Savior. It is there, at the feet of Jesus, you will find an inexhaustible source of strength, incomprehensible grace, unfathomable depths of love, and forgiveness that is unending.

These messages are meant to encourage, comfort, and uplift no matter the season of life in which you find yourself. May they be a healing balm to all who read them, saturating even the deepest wounds with the love, grace, and forgiveness of Christ. May they embolden you to enter the very throne room of God, for it is there you will come face-to-face with love incarnate and find all that you need.

1

Identity

Deuteronomy 33:12 (NIV)
Let the beloved of the LORD rest secure in him,
for he shields him all day long and the one the
LORD loves rests between his shoulders.

Ephesians 1:18–19 (NIV)
I pray that the eyes of your heart may be enlightened in
order that you may know the hope to which he has called
you, the riches of his glorious inheritance in his holy people,
and his incomparably great power for us who believe.

As I look back over the years, recalling conversations with fellow sisters in Christ, as well as my own thoughts about life, I see a common thread. As women of God, we struggle to embrace our identity in Christ. We struggle to believe who He says we are as His new creation. On one hand, we believe because we know God's Word is inspired by the Holy Spirit and is therefore inerrant. On the other hand, we waver believing His truths and promises are for everyone but us. Bound by past hurts, buried by present failures, and fearful of who we have or have not become, our vision can become clouded, making it difficult to see who we truly are.

I long to see myself as God does—to see myself through His eyes. I know I am not alone here. And I fear if we are unable to see ourselves as He does and truly take hold of who we are in Christ and the freedom He has purchased for us through His blood, we will never truly grow. We will never live the life He intends for us. We will never know the depth of His grace or His riches, which are ours, and the freedom He has to set us free. We will journey through this life stunted in our growth, never knowing Him as He wants to be known, never reaching the full potential He has created in us and planned for us, forever living a half-life devoid of the joy, peace, and rest that can be found in Him alone.

Help us, Lord, Your daughters, to see ourselves through Your eyes, to believe we are Your beloved, to know with all our hearts we are the ones whom Jesus loves—at all times, in every way, without condition, and without limit. Give us faith to believe beyond a shadow of a doubt that we, Your blood-bought daughters, are covered in the righteousness of Christ and therefore without blemish, spot, or stain in Your sight. Help us to remember that You see us as pure and holy, washed in the blood of our Savior, and forever cleansed of our sins and unrighteousness. Therefore, we are and will forever be precious in Your sight.

In Jesus's name, we pray. Amen.

2

Repentance

Deuteronomy 7:8 (NIV)
It was because the LORD loved you … that he brought
you out with a mighty hand and redeemed you.

Last week, we discussed embracing our true identity in Christ
and His promise that we are a new creation dwelt by His very Spirit.
In light of that truth, we are called to be "dead to sin but alive to
God in Christ Jesus" (Rom. 6:11 [NIV]). While we should seek to
obey this command daily with all of our heart, mind, and strength,
we also need to remember that we will never attain the perfect
sinless nature of Christ.

Therefore, when you do sin, remember: "While we were still sinners,
Christ died for us" (Rom. 5:8 [NKJV]). Go to Him. Acknowledge
and confess it immediately. Repent, ask God for His forgiveness, and
receive it. Don't allow shame to keep you from going to Him. This
will only allow the enemy to gain a foothold in your life. Confessing
our sins to the Lord regularly keeps sin from taking root in our
hearts and spreading like an infection to every area of our life.

Remember: your life has been redeemed at an unfathomable price. The Father gave everything so you could be forgiven and restored to Him. He will never get fed up with forgiving you. You do not have to fear Him ever turning you away because He has had enough of you and your pleas for forgiveness. He is not surprised by your failings. And He is always ready to forgive. However, He also wants you and me to remember we are no longer slaves to sin and its power. Instead, we have the power of Christ in us, enabling us to overcome. Therefore, let us live daily in the power and sufficiency of Christ!

3

Expectations

Romans 3:23–24 (ESV)
For all have sinned and fall short of the glory
of God, and are justified by his grace as a gift,
through the redemption that is in Christ Jesus.

As women, I think often our tendency is to want things to
be just so—our marriages, children, friendships, church life, and
careers, for example. While we should want the best in every aspect
of our lives and give our best to every relationship in it, the reality
is *life is messy; people are messy; relationships are messy.* They will
always consist of two or more flawed, sinful human beings who will
inevitably fall short of our expectations, including ourselves. Life,
nor the people in it, will never fit into our perfect plan.

We can even apply this mentality to our own relationship with the
Lord. Often, we want our relationship with Him to look and feel a
certain way. When it does not, some are met with disappointment,
maybe even bitterness, driving them away from Him in anger or
frustration. Others may believe it is a result of something lacking in
themselves. They simply are not enough and will never be enough.

We believe the lie that unless we reach the standard of perfection we have set up for ourselves, the Lord will not bless us. *But the truth is, my friends, you will never get your ducks in a row. None of us will.*

We mature in our relationship with Him over time. And He conforms us more and more into His image and likeness, but we will never get it right. We will never quite be where we want to be or have it together as well as we would like. But God does not ask us to get it together before He blesses us. His decision to bless us is not contingent upon our works, whether good or bad. He blesses us because we are His children, and it pleases Him to do so. If it appears He is withholding a blessing or an answer to prayer, it is because He has a greater purpose in doing so—not because you have not earned it or prayed hard enough for it. "For by grace you have been saved through faith. And this is not your own doing; it is the gift of God, not a result of works, so that no one may boast" (Eph. 2:8–9 [ESV]).

4

Decision-Making

Proverbs 24:3–4 (AMP)
Through [skillful and godly] wisdom a house [a life, a home, a family] is built, and by understanding it is established [on a sound and good foundation], and by knowledge its rooms are filled with all precious and pleasant riches.

I think we can all agree life is hard. However, I cannot even fathom what my life would look like if I did not know Jesus, if I could not seek Him daily for the wisdom needed to go about my everyday life. Think of the number of decisions we must make in a day, let alone a week, a month, or a year. Decisions about the smallest occurrences to the most significant achievements all have an impact on us and those around us, especially those in our own homes and those who are closest to us. Each day, we see how the wisdom of the world is destroying relationships, marriages, and families.

"This wisdom does not descend from above, but is earthly, sensual, demonic" (James 3:15, NKJV).

In stark contrast, God's Word also tells us, "The wisdom from above is first of all pure. It is also peace loving, gentle at all times, and willing to yield to others. It is full of mercy and the fruit of good deeds. It shows no favoritism and is always sincere" (James 3:17 [NKJV]).

The only way our lives, marriages, families, and homes can be built up and sustained through the ever-changing seasons of life is through the wisdom we receive from God's Word and our personal prayer time with Him. Let us be women who are committed to making these both a priority in our everyday lives, not ones who go about our days in our own strength and wisdom, so we may thrive amid a culture that is decaying and collapsing all around us, for God's Word says, "Unless the LORD builds the house, they labor in vain who build it" (Ps. 127:1 [NKJV]).

Next, we see it is understanding that gives us a sure and strong foundation where we can grow. I think part of this understanding refers to God's Word. Reading, studying, and memorizing scripture are vital for our spiritual growth and our ability to live according to God's Word. Without it, we are just treading water. It gives us insight and understanding into His design for our relationships as wife, mother, friend, and fellow servant of Christ. It is when we are functioning within these parameters that we find ourselves standing on a secure foundation. But I believe there also must be a personal level of understanding in each of our relationships. There must be a desire and a willingness to know our spouses, children, friends, and those whom we serve alongside of for there to be true understanding and connectedness—an environment where each person can flourish.

We all have a longing to be seen, heard, and understood. Yet so many feel anything but. I realize this is no easy task. It truly is a labor of love, which requires more patience, time, and energy than we generally want to give—if we are honest. But let us be those who seek to do unto others what we want done to us (Matt. 7:12). Let us pray and ask God to give us hearts that are steadfast in their pursuit to understand and obey His Word, as well as an unwavering commitment to stop, listen, and truly get to know and understand those with whom we share our lives.

Last, it is the knowledge and wisdom we gain by taking the time and energy required to love others well that fill the rooms of our hearts, our homes, our churches, and our workplaces with precious and pleasant riches. To honor another by deeming them worthy of being seen, known, and loved is an incredible blessing, one that brings a brightened countenance to their face and a pleasantness to their life. Through it, we are extending Christ's love and grace to them in a tangible way—a way in which, I believe, most would be eager to turn around and share with others. Only God knows how far the ripple effects may reach and how many generations could be impacted by a genuine desire to seek wisdom, understanding, and knowledge.

5

Intercession

Psalm 17:8 (NKJV)
Keep me as the apple of Your eye; Hide me
under the shadow of Your wings.

As I sit here considering what to write, I am reminded of an account in Exodus 17:8–17. The Israelites went to battle, and Moses stood at the top of a hill to pray, hands raised, holding the rod of God. But the battle raged long, and his hands became so heavy that it was difficult to keep them raised to the Lord. Therefore, Aaron and Hur put a rock under him so he could sit down. Then they both supported his hands, standing on each side of Moses so that his hands were steady until sundown.

And that, my dear sisters in Christ, is what our prayers can do for one another. We may not always be able to come alongside someone in a practical way to help them through a strenuous and burdensome season of life. Yet we can do so spiritually. We can lift one another up in prayer, asking the Lord to strengthen them when they feel weak, sustain them when they feel weary, and to carry them on days they feel they have nothing left to give. We can pray that they find, in

Jesus, the rest He assures to those who come to Him when they are weary and heavy burdened (Matt. 11:28).

Our commitment to pray for others reassures that they are not forgotten. They have not been abandoned. It is a reminder that they are deeply loved by the eternal God, who has engraved them on the palms of His hands (Isa. 49:16).

6

Compassion

Psalm 145:8 (NKJV)
The LORD is gracious and full of compassion,
slow to anger and great in mercy.

At times, I can take for granted that I attend an incredible church with solid biblical teaching from a pastor who clearly loves both the Lord and the flock he has been given to teach, lead, and oversee. He takes his stewardship seriously and teaches the Word of God in truth and love. However, this is not everyone's experience. Not all pastors and church leaders "correctly handle the word of truth" (2 Tim. 2:15 [NIV]). Sadly, there are churches that use the Word of God to control, manipulate, instill fear, and take advantage of God's people. There are leaders that teach that any kind of pain or suffering in your life is a result of a lack of faith or unconfessed sin in your life. There are congregations that focus mainly on passages of scripture that speak of punishment and judgment to frighten people into obeying God, teaching that if they do not, they will be punished and/or abandoned by God.

Sadly, this has been the experience of my friend. Many years of such teaching has instilled in her an unhealthy fear of God. She once shared that anytime she hears or reads something that says "God commands ...," she physically cringes. The word *commands* conjures up for her a visual of God's anger even when the command is followed by things such as "be of good courage" or "do not fear." Those are loving commands, followed by promises of God's presence and provision in our lives. But that is not the teaching that she has received. She recalled being in a Sunday school class where they were talking about Jesus's commands, and someone said, "God will crush you if you don't obey!" I was both stunned and heartbroken when I heard this. But I wonder, how many others have received similar teaching? How many others have been deceived into believing similar lies about God and His character? How many of us may not agree with such a harsh statement but still, maybe unintentionally, believe or behave in a way that says our acceptance before God is based on some merit of our own?

While God has many attributes, and we should not focus so much on one that we neglect the others, what I see strewn throughout the pages of scripture is His compassion. I have experienced His great compassion in my own life and know its ability to bring healing. I have struggled and suffered to such an extent for so long that God has instilled in me a deep compassion for others who are also struggling and suffering. For those of you to whom this applies, I want to encourage you and remind you of God's compassion for you in His Word. I know at times it can be easy to lose sight of. I pray the truths and promises I have included below will be a comfort to you. For those of you who may not be struggling yourselves but know someone who is going through a difficult time, I hope you will share these scriptures with them to remind them of God's faithfulness and compassion toward His children:

Psalm 86:15 (NKJV)
But You, O LORD, are a God full of compassion, and gracious, longsuffering and abundant in mercy and truth.

Psalm 111:4 (NKJV)
He has made His wonderful works to be remembered; The LORD is gracious and full of compassion.

Psalm 135:14 (NKJV)
For the LORD will judge His people, and He will have compassion on His servants.

Lamentations 3:22 (NKJV)
Through the LORD's mercies we are not consumed, because His compassions fail not.

Zechariah 7:9 (NKJV)
Thus says the LORD of hosts: "Execute true justice, show mercy and compassion everyone to his brother."

Micah 7:19 (NKJV)
He will again have compassion on us, and will subdue our iniquities. You will cast all our sins into the depths of the sea.

Matthew 9:36 (NKJV)
But when He saw the multitudes, He was moved with compassion for them, because they were weary and scattered, like sheep having no shepherd.

Matthew 14:14 (NKJV)
And when Jesus went out He saw a great multitude; and He was moved with compassion for them, and healed their sick.

This is by no means an exhaustive list; however, I pray it drives home the truth of His love for you.

7

Praying God's Word

Exodus 33:13 (NLT)
If it is true that you look favorably on me, let me
know your ways so I may understand you more
fully and continue to enjoy your favor.

When I read this, everything in me screams, "Yes, Lord! Amen!
Let it be so!" I am a big fan of reading passages of scripture in
multiple versions to get a more well-rounded understanding of what
it is saying. When I read this version recently, it was as if I was
reading this verse for the first time. In so many words, this has been a
prayer of mine for so long. But to see it worded in this particular way
really spoke to me. I thought, *Yes, Lord, this is my prayer; this is what
my heart longs for.* Now that I have these words from scripture, I will
be praying His Word back to Him and waiting for Him to answer.

Do you ever pray God's word back to Him? Do you ask Him for the
things He says we should ask for? Do you remind yourself of His
promises as you pray about specific requests or circumstances? Do
you come in agreement with the truths that Jesus taught us during
His earthly ministry and those written by the men who penned the

scriptures, inspired by the Holy Spirit? I believe it is good for us to pray God's Word back to Him—to let His Word be the foundation for our prayers. It shows God we value His Word and want to live according to it. It helps us to continually renew our minds with the truth and experience its transforming power in our lives. It also helps us to hide His Word in our heart that we may not sin against Him (Ps. 119:11).

If this is not something you do, give it try. If it is something you already do, maybe try being intentional about doing it a few extra times a day or week and watch how it changes your prayer life and your relationship with the Lord. The more of a habit it becomes, the more second nature it will be. "Blessed [fortunate, prosperous, and favored by God] is the man who does not walk in the counsel of the wicked [following their advice and example], nor stand in the path of sinners, nor sit [down to rest] in the seat of scoffers (ridiculers). But his delight is in the law of the LORD, and on His law [His precepts and teachings] he [habitually] meditates day and night. And he will be like a tree firmly planted [and fed] by streams of water, which yields its fruit in its season; Its leaf does not wither; And whatever he does, he prospers [and comes to maturity]" (Ps. 1:1–3 [AMP]).

8

Protection and Provision

Psalm 36:7 (AMP)
How precious is your lovingkindness, O God! The children
of men take refuge in the shadow of Your wings.

I recently came across a picture of a mother swan and all her
cygnets tucked under the protection of her wing. I was deeply moved
by this image. Immediately, I recalled the scriptures that speak of
finding refuge under the shadow of God's wings. Instead of writing
this week, I felt led to simply share these scriptures and let God speak
to each of your hearts individually as He knows you need. There
are seven scripture references including today's verse. I pray you will
take one verse each day this week and spend time considering what
it says. Sit quietly before Lord, asking Him to speak to your heart
regarding each one of these precious promises, and praise Him for
His faithful love that covers you.

Psalm 91:4 (NIV)
He will cover you with his feathers, and under his wings you will find refuge; His faithfulness will be your shield and rampart.

Deuteronomy 32:11 (NLT)
Like an eagle that rouses her chicks and hovers over her young, so he spread his wings to take them up and carried them safely on his pinions.

Psalm 17:7–8 (AMP)
Wondrously show Your [marvelous and amazing] lovingkindness, O Savior of those who take refuge at Your right hand from those who rise up against them. Keep me [in Your affectionate care, protect me] as the apple of Your eye; Hide me in the [protective] shadow of Your wings.

Psalm 57:1 (NLT)
Have mercy on me, O God, have mercy! I look to you for protection. I will hide beneath the shadow of your wings until the danger passes by.

Psalm 61:1–4 (ESV)
Hear my cry, O God, listen to my prayer; from the end of the earth I call to you when my heart is faint. Lead me to the rock that is higher than I, for you have been my refuge, a strong tower against the enemy. Let me dwell in your tent forever! Let me take refuge under the shelter of your wings! Selah

Psalm 63:7 (ESV)
For you have been my help, and in the shadow of your wings I will sing for joy.

9

Purpose

Psalm 57:2 (NLT)
I cry out to God Most High, to God who
will fulfill his purpose for me.

Have you ever had the Lord communicate something to you—a promise to be fulfilled, a specific calling on your life, or a particular plan that He intends to accomplish, yet, when you look at your life those things seem to be an impossibility? You cannot imagine how you are going to get from here to there, from now to then; the chasm too wide, the distance too far, the obstacles too great to overcome. That word from the Lord is like a mountain that stands off in the distance, insurmountable. In such times, we need to remind ourselves that "He who promised is faithful" (Heb. 10:23 [ESV]). It is in God's grace that He gives us that word, that glimpse, that hope for the future. Otherwise, we may grow weary from the journey and all the difficulties that it brings and give up hope.

But if we are willing to labor in prayer, we gradually strengthen our spiritual muscles and build the perseverance needed to be "constantly rejoicing in hope [because of our confidence in Christ], steadfast and patient in distress, devoted to prayer [continually seeking wisdom, guidance, and strength]" (Rom. 12:12 [AMP]). As a result, our faith is strengthened and our hope continually renewed as we trust in both God's ability and His faithfulness to bring about what He has promised.

However, maybe you are in a season where your faith is faltering and your hope is all but shattered, leaving a void of hopelessness where there was once anticipation and expectation of a promise fulfilled. Maybe your spiritual muscles are weak and withered, making it difficult to pray. Please know that God sees you and is filled with compassion for you. He understands your weakness and is gracious to you. In Psalm 119, we see the psalmist reminding God of His promise and finding renewed strength and hope according to His Word. Verses 49–50 state, "Remember [always] the word and promise to Your servant, in which You have made me hope. This is my comfort in my affliction, that Your word has revived me and given me life" (AMP). I would encourage you to join in this prayer. Do not be afraid to humbly remind the Lord of His promises and ask Him to revive you, your faith, and your hope according to His Word.

Whatever season you are in, remember that God's faithfulness to His promises is not dependent on you but on Him alone. As our verse for today's devotion tells us, it is God who fulfills His purpose for us. Our part is to worship and praise Him for who He is and to trust that He is moving mightily on our behalf whether we can see it or not. May the scriptures below be an encouragement and comfort to your hearts.

> Romans 4:18 (NIV)
> Against all hope, Abraham in hope believed and so became the father of many nations, just as it had been said to him.

Psalm 33:20 (NIV)
We wait in hope for the LORD; he is our help and
our shield.

Romans 15:13 (NIV)
May the God of hope fill you with all joy and peace
as you trust in him, so that you may overflow with
hope by the power of the Holy Spirit.

10

Holy Spirit

Romans 5:5 (ESV)
God's love has been poured out into our hearts
through the Holy Spirit, who has been given to us.

I was asked by a friend about the role of the Holy Spirit and whether we should be praying to Him. Let me start out by saying, I am no theologian. But this response is a prayerful one and a personal one. Those of you reading these devotions are varied in background, denomination, and where you are in your walk with the Lord. However, my hope and prayer are that all of you will benefit from this response in some way.

There is only one God, but He is triune: Father, Son, and Holy Spirit. Therefore, each is fully God: God the Father, God the Son, and God the Holy Spirit. While each is fully and equally God, they are different in role; God the father being the head.

Because each person of the Trinity is God, yes, we are able and, I believe, encouraged to pray to each person according to our needs. Sometimes when I pray, I address Him as God or Lord, and I am not thinking about the individual persons of the Godhead. But there are also many times when I do. For example, when I am praying about something regarding God's sovereignty over situations and circumstances, a need or longing for His provision, or wisdom regarding the future, I pray to the Father.

Then there are times I pray specifically to Jesus. Because He is our Savior, I often pray to Him for protection in certain situations, also for guidance and discernment in daily decision-making as things come up throughout the day. I go to Him for comfort and refuge, trusting that He is sheltering me under the shadow of His wings. I go to Him for strength in times of weakness and help to live according to His Word and His teaching so I may live a life that reflects His character. Likewise, I pray that His light would shine through me to all I encounter day to day—that they would see Him and not me.

I also pray specifically to the Holy Spirit. He is the very Spirit of God in us to guide us in our daily walk. Every thought, every decision, every word—He is there to guide, direct, and instruct us according to the will of the Father. I pray to Him for those very things: wisdom for each day, wisdom as I read the Word and how to apply it to my life, wisdom about how to spend my time each day, wisdom in my interactions with others. There is a verse that I have often prayed from the book of Isaiah. In it, the Lord says, "Whether you turn to the right or to the left, your ears will hear a voice behind you, saying, 'This is the way; walk in it'" (Isa. 30:21 [NIV]). This is what I want—in every moment of my life to be walking according to God's will. Unfortunately, my hearing is not always so good. While this is my desire and my prayer, I don't always feel as confident as I would like regarding these things. However, there are times when I am seeking His wisdom and direction, and I truly sense that He is right there speaking to my heart and guiding me along the way. But there are also times I need to prayerfully step out in faith not knowing what the end result will be.

The Spirit also convicts us when we step outside of God's will and when we sin. He directs us back to the Father, so we can repent and receive His forgiveness and grace. He then gets us back up on our feet and moving, all the while continually interceding before the Father on our behalf. Because He is the Spirit of God, He knows the will of God and is always praying according to it on our behalf, especially when we are in a place where we do not know how we should be praying for ourselves or our circumstances (Rom. 8:1–27). Likewise, Romans 8:34 says that Jesus Himself is in heaven also interceding for us at the right hand of the Father.

Last, the Spirit is given to us as a seal of our inheritance in God's kingdom. Ephesians 1:13–14 declare, "You also were included in Christ when you heard the message of truth, the gospel of your salvation. When you believed you were marked in him with a seal, the promised Holy Spirit, who is a deposit guaranteeing our inheritance until the redemption of those who are God's possession to the praise of His glory" (NIV). In addition, "The Spirit Himself bears witness with our spirit that we are children of God" (Rom. 8:16 [NKJV]). Therefore, do not let anyone cause you to doubt the permanency and absoluteness of your salvation. If you have truly given your life to Christ, acknowledging Him as Savior and Lord, and have received His forgiveness, you belong to Him. You are saved. You are sealed. Ready to be delivered into the very presence of God when He calls you home. The Holy Spirit is the blessed assurance of our place in God's family, made possible through the finished work of Jesus on the cross and given to us by our heavenly Father.

11

Suffering

John 16:33 (NLT)
I have told you all of this so that you may have peace in
me. Here on earth you will have many trials and sorrows.
But take heart, because I have overcome the world.

Revelation 21:4 (NLT)
He will wipe away every tear from their eyes, and
there will be no more death or sorrow or crying
or pain. All these things are gone forever.

At times, life can be unkind, realities harsh, and circumstances
unbearable. But that does not mean that God is callous or unloving.
God has not promised to spare us from suffering. Instead, His Word
tells us that we will have trouble in this world (John 16:33). But
He has also assured us that His very presence will be with us in it
and through it every step of the way. God tells us, "When you pass
through the waters, I will be with you; and when you pass through
the rivers, they will not sweep over you. When you walk through
the fire, you will not be burned; the flames will not set you ablaze"
(Isa. 43:2 [NIV]). As if the promise of His presence with us was not

enough, God gives us even more by promising that our suffering never goes to waste. His Word even goes as far as to say, "We can rejoice when we run into problems and trials, for we know that they help us develop endurance. And endurance develops strength of character, and character strengthens our confident hope of salvation" (Rom. 5:3–4 [NLT]). Although, I will admit, on more than one occasion I have found myself saying, "Lord, I don't think this is taking place in me."

I am no stranger to suffering. The last seven years alone have brought an indescribable level of debilitating pain from a chronic health condition and four years of seemingly endless surgeries, each followed by long and painful recovery periods, not to mention profound loneliness and a sense of loss as the world around me moves and the people around me live as I have sat watching from a window, often unable to take part in it all. I have thought to myself, *Lord, You say that suffering produces endurance, character, and hope, but I don't think it's true for me. I don't ever seem to get there. I still feel so lacking in strength and Christ-like character in the face of suffering. I have stumbled into the grip of hopelessness time and again. I feel so far from who You have called me to be.*

It is then that He lovingly reminds me, "For those who love God all things work together for good, for those who are called according to his purpose" (Rom. 8:28 [NIV]). These experiences and many more have made me who I am today. While it's true these things have had negative effects, they have also worked in me for good. The comfort I have received from God in my own suffering I can now share with others who are also suffering. The Bible says, "All praise to God, the Father of our Lord Jesus Christ. God is our merciful Father and the source of all comfort. He comforts us in all our troubles so that we can comfort others. When they are troubled, we will be able to give them the same comfort God has given us" (2 Cor. 1:3–4 [NLT]).

Without a personal understanding of suffering, it's difficult to relate to others in their suffering. Suffering enables us to be empathetic toward people in a unique way, especially when we've experienced similar trials. Shared suffering enables you to come alongside another—to shed tears together, mourn together, or simply sit in silence together. It brings about genuine, heartfelt prayer and intercession for one another that floods the throne room of God. Therefore, from our suffering, God produces a double blessing.

My friends, compassion, understanding, and empathy are some of the greatest gifts you could ever give someone. Be generous in your giving of them! And let us also encourage one another with the promise that in the end, when our time has come or Jesus returns for His bride, the Church, He will bring us into eternal glory, where there will be no more death, sorrow, crying or pain (Rev. 21:4).

12

Shame

Exodus 15:2–3 (NIV)
The LORD is my strength and my defense; he has
become my salvation. He is my God, and I will praise
him … The LORD is a warrior; the LORD is his name.

Is anyone sick of running or hiding? Is anyone else wondering
why we still do this when we know better? Is this still our default
response thousands of years since it first occurred in the Garden of
Eden? Yes … I do not know why, but yes … even now, after Christ
has come and sacrificed Himself on our behalf, having paid for
our sins so we could freely receive forgiveness and be restored to
the Father; even still we tend to run from Him in guilt and shame
instead of running to Him when we sin. Shame sets in, not only
when we sin but also when others sin against us. Either way, we allow
it to fester. Then the lies of the enemy start seeping into our wounds
and spread like an infection. We know what we need—whether it be
forgiveness for our own sins, forgiveness of others who have sinned
against us, purification of our hearts and minds from the lies of the
enemy, or all the above. Yet our innate sense of guilt and shame so
often keep us from the only one who can restore and renew us.

However, God is not content to leave us wandering in the dark bound by our sin and shame. There is no place we can run from Him that is too high or so far that His eye is not continually on us, nor His presence continually pursuing us, as He beckons us back to Himself with love and forgiveness. His will and sovereign purpose for our individual lives will not allow us to remain hiding behind the walls we have built to guard ourselves—walls of fear, rejection, and isolation. His unconditional, unfathomable, and unending love will not permit us to stay buried under the shame of our past or present, nor bound by the lies of the enemy.

Praise God today for His relentless pursuit of you—His love fights to take hold of you to heal and restore you.

13

Strongholds

Psalm 40:1–2 (AMP)
I waited patiently and expectantly for the LORD; and
He inclined to me and heard my cry. He brought me
up out of a horrible pit [of tumult and of destruction],
out of the miry clay, and He set my feet upon a rock,
steadying my footsteps and establishing my path.

I hope you were able to spend time over the last week renewing
your mind with God's Word that speaks of His love for you, how He
fights for you, and His faithfulness toward you. However, I realize
that some beliefs and mindsets are so deeply ingrained that, while
we want nothing more than to believe the truth wholeheartedly, the
lies that we have believed have been our "truth" for so long that it
can take time to undo the damage and destruction that they have
left in their wake.

When it seems as though nearly everything and everyone in your
life reinforces such feelings, these feelings can become beliefs. They
become part of our identity and invade every crack and crevice of
our lives—every thought, every word, every action. They influence

every relationship, even that with our Heavenly Father. Yet, if we are indwelt with the Spirit of God, then we are filled with the Word of God because Jesus Himself is the Word become flesh (John 1:1), and it is His Spirit that lives in us. As we see above, the Bible encourages us to continually call upon the Lord, to wait patiently and expectantly for Him to draw us out of the pit of tumult and destruction and set us in a secure place where we can stand firm.

I looked up the definitions for tumult and destruction, wanting a deeper understanding of what these verses are conveying.

> Tumult: highly distressing agitation of mind or feeling; turbulent mental or emotional disturbance

> Destruction: the condition of being destroyed; demolition; annihilation

The feelings of shame, self-hatred, and worthlessness; fear of being rejected, unwanted, unlovable, and without value to anyone are highly distressing. They cause both mental and emotional disturbance. Allowing these things to be the foundation and substance of our identity instead of Christ is destructive—not a quick and total destruction but a slow, continual process of being destroyed, a demolition that tears down one part at a time until we are no longer recognizable. We, His blood-bought daughters, created to live abundantly through Christ's sufficiency—to reflect His character to the world around us and proclaim His power to save, forgive, and transform—can lose our witness for Christ, not our salvation but the purpose for which we were made and saved, which is, first and foremost, to glorify God; second, to share His gospel message of love, forgiveness, and hope to those from the end of our streets to the ends of the earth. "Therefore do not cast away your confidence, which has great reward" (Heb. 10:35 [NKJV]).

There is a spiritual battle going on behind the scenes to gain territory in our hearts and minds. Satan wants nothing more than to render us ineffective for the kingdom of God. In 2 Corinthians 10:4–5, we learn that "the weapons we fight with are not the weapons of the world. On the contrary, they have divine power to demolish strongholds. We demolish arguments and every pretension that sets itself up against the knowledge of God, and we take captive every thought to make it obedient to Christ" (NIV). Do you see that? Through the power of Christ, we can demolish the strongholds in our life, rendering them powerless. When we stay connected to the Vine—that is, Jesus—the only demolition taking place in our lives is of what contradicts the Word of God. Furthermore, it is credited to us as righteousness when we believe what God says of us. Therefore, let us choose to be women of faith, affirming, we believe, Lord, help our unbelief! (Mark 9:24)

14

Spiritual Gifts

Romans 12:4–8 (NIV)
For just as each of us has one body with many members,
and these members do not all have the same function,
so in Christ we, though many, form one body, and each
member belongs to all the others. We have different
gifts, according to the grace given to each one of us.

We know from God's Word that once we are saved and indwelt
with God's Spirit, we are each given gifts to serve God and His
people; furthermore, to reach the world around us and draw them to
Christ. Maybe you are someone who knows their gifts and strengths.
If so, praise God! It is a blessing to know your God-given gifts and
strengths and how you can use them for His glory and His purposes.
Though I think there are many people who do not have such clarity.
They long to fulfill His purposes for their life but struggle to discern
His will and their gifting. They feel their path is hidden and their
gifts altogether unknown. Still, others, deep in their hearts, question
whether they truly have any gifts to serve God and others well. Let
me take a moment here to say, that is a lie from the enemy. Trust in
the promise of God that He has given each one of His children gifts,

and He has a particular plan and purpose in doing so. You are not the exception. "God is not a human, that he should lie, not a human being, that he should change his mind. Does he speak and then not act? Does he promise and not fulfill?" (Num. 23:19 [NIV]).

I have spent years asking the Lord to show me my gifts and strengths and how He would have me use them for His glory, the furtherance of His kingdom, the blessing of His people, and the salvation of the lost in our world. His response? Silence ... years of silence on the matter except for a still, small voice whispering to my heart to trust that He has a unique plan and purpose for my life, as He does for each one of us. In more recent years, God has helped me to recognize the joy I feel in speaking truth, life, love, and compassion into the lives of others in a personal way. It is my heart's desire to come alongside of others—to connect, support, encourage, and lift them up. It is what fills me up. It is what makes me feel alive. It is a gift He has given me to use for His purposes. On the other hand, I have deeply entrenched trust issues that often keep people at a distance, making it difficult to do the things I long to do—to have real relationships where I can be vulnerable yet safe. Maybe that is why there is so much spiritual warfare in my mind and heart regarding relational issues.

As I touched on last week, Satan does not want God's people to thrive, to fulfill His purposes, or to share the love, forgiveness, and freedom of Christ to those who are lost and broken. He wants nothing more than to keep us incapacitated so we are not a threat to his schemes to blind and deceive the multitudes. He also wants to keep God's people from living their lives in the fullness of Christ, the power of His resurrection, and being continually formed into His image—the image that Satan so greatly despises.

Sadly, I have allowed him a foothold in my life amid pain and suffering, both past and present. At times, I have hardened my heart toward others and even toward God in ways. But God has forgiven me and shown me that my sins and failures have not disqualified me from being used by Him. He knows my heart and that my desire is to know Him, to love Him more deeply, and to serve Him more fully. His desire is to use me despite my doubt, fear, confusion, and selfishness, which so often holds me back. The same is true for you. Whatever your story, whatever your shortcomings, whatever your failures, you have not been disqualified. God is greater than them all. Even when we are unfaithful, He is faithful—faithful to forgive, to cleanse us from all unrighteousness, to place our feet upon the rock, and to fill us afresh with His Spirit, enabling us to do the work that He has prepared in advance for us to do (Eph. 2:10).

15

WEEK

Body of Christ

Proverbs 18:24 (NIV)
One who has unreliable friends soon comes to ruin,
but there is a friend who sticks closer than a brother.

I would like to encourage you this week to spend time each day considering what an incredible gift it is to be part of the body of Christ. Take time to recall the ways God has provided for you and cared for you through another member of His body. I would even encourage you to keep a running list throughout the week, jotting things down as they come to mind. My hope is that recalling the blessings of God will bring forth praise to God each day. I would also encourage you to intentionally set aside time at the end of the week in worship and praise of your heavenly Father for calling you His own, making you a part of His family, and for the abundant blessings that He has poured into your life as a result.

I recently recalled a time I was at a social event, a time that was meant to be a celebration. Yet, as I sat there surrounded by others, I felt alone, out of place, uncomfortable, and unwanted. Then, out of the blue, I got an email from a friend. This friend had no idea where

37

I was, what was going on, or how I was feeling at that very moment. I opened the email to read, "I am praying for you. When I wake at night, I pray for you. In the morning as I get ready, I pray for you. In between, I lift you up." My eyes instantly filled with tears—not tears of the sadness I had been feeling but an overwhelming sense of love and genuine care from this dear friend and sister in Christ, a stark contrast to what I was presently surrounded with. This sweet and timely message made the rest of the night bearable, knowing that my friend, who lives halfway across the country, cares so much for me that she thinks of and prays for me regularly. That environment where I felt so alone was now far less burdensome.

I was in awe of how God provided for me through my sister in Christ that night. He knew my need and put me on her heart at that very moment to comfort me. "For we are members of His body," and "from him the whole body, joined and held together by every supporting ligament, grows and builds itself up in love, as each part does its work" (Eph. 5:30, 4:16 [NIV]). This is only one example of the countless ways in which God has used His people to bless me and provide for my needs, both spiritual and physical. When I take time to think about these things, my heart cannot help but overflow with gratitude and thanksgiving to our Almighty Father, who knows our needs before we even ask Him (Matt. 6:8).

16

Praise

Psalm 118:22–24 (NLT)
The stone that the builders rejected has now become
the cornerstone. This is the LORD's doing, and
it is wonderful to see. This is the day the LORD
has made. We will rejoice and be glad in it.

Let us determine together that this week will be one full of praise to our Savior! "Sing to the LORD a new song; sing to the LORD, all the earth. Sing to the LORD, praise his name; proclaim his salvation day after day" (Ps. 96:1–2 [NIV]). I cannot wait till the day we are all standing around the throne of God together, worshipping Jesus, the Lamb who was slain, and singing His praise with one voice together with all the angels! That day cannot come soon enough! But it *is* coming!

May our hearts and minds maintain a posture of praise and worship of our Savior. To encourage you, I wanted to share these scriptures— that they may deepen your worship and elevate your praise according to His Word; that He may receive the utmost glory and praise!

I hope you will read and pray through each of these verses this week. Lift up your hearts! Lift up your hands! Lift up your voices! He is the King of kings and the Lord of lords; our Savior and our God! Pour out your hearts in praise!

1 Peter 1:8–9 (NLT)
You love him even though you have never seen him. Though you do not see him now, you trust him; and you rejoice with a glorious, inexpressible joy. The reward for trusting him will be the salvation of your souls.

Psalm 147:1, 3–5 (NLT)
Praise the LORD! How good to sing praises to our God! How delightful and how fitting! He heals the brokenhearted and bandages their wounds. He counts the stars and calls them all by name. How great is our LORD! His power is absolute! His understanding is beyond comprehension!

Psalm 148:1–5 (NLT)
Praise the LORD! Praise the LORD from the heavens! Praise him from the skies! Praise him, all his angels! Praise him, all the armies of heaven! Praise him, sun and moon! Praise him, all you twinkling stars! Praise him, skies above! Praise him, vapors high above the clouds! Let every created thing give praise to the LORD.

Psalm 150:1–6 (NLT)
Praise the LORD! Praise God in his sanctuary; praise him in his mighty heaven! Praise him for his mighty works; praise his unequaled greatness! Praise him with a blast of the ram's horn; praise

him with the lyre and harp! Praise him with the tambourine and dancing; praise him with strings and flutes! Praise him with a clash of cymbals; praise him with loud clanging cymbals. Let everything that breathes sing praises to the LORD! Praise the LORD!

Ephesians 3:20–21 (AMP)
Now to Him who is able to [carry out His purpose and] do superabundantly more than all that we dare ask or think [infinitely beyond our greatest prayers, hopes, or dreams], according to His power that is at work within us, to Him be the glory in the church and in Christ Jesus throughout all generations forever and ever. Amen.

Psalm 57:10–11 (NLT)
For your unfailing love is as high as the heavens. Your faithfulness reaches to the clouds. Be exalted, O God, above the highest heavens. May your glory shine over all the earth.

Psalm 66:1–4 (NLT)
Shout joyful praises to God, all the earth! Sing about the glory of his name! Tell the world how glorious he is. Say to God, "How awesome are your deeds! Your enemies cringe before your mighty power. Everything on earth will worship you; they will sing your praises, shouting your name in glorious songs."

17

Discernment

Proverbs 12:25 (NIV)
Anxiety weighs down the heart, but a kind word cheers it up.

Have you ever been Bible shamed by someone? a pastor or church leader? someone in your congregation? maybe a trusted friend and sister in Christ? It cuts to the core, doesn't it? Why is it that people think this approach works? How does one feel justified in taking the precious, eternal, and holy Word of God and using it to cut down and heap shame and guilt on a person for whom Christ died to set free from that very shame and guilt?

Fighting feelings of shame is a regular battleground for me. I know who I am in Christ, and I know that "it is for freedom that I have been set free" (Gal. 5:1). I know I am washed, cleansed, and purified in the blood of my Savior. But it is an area where I still struggle. An area where I still need healing and deliverance. There was a particular season in my life when I was struggling deeply with a profound sense of shame. At that time, I had regular interactions with a particular person; and each time after hearing this person's words, I went home with my head hanging lower than when I came in.

My friends, this should never be so. No one should ever leave our presence feeling as though we have created, reinforced, or contributed to a sense of shame they may feel in themselves. That experience scarred me for years and affected every relationship I had, even that with God. Yet He was so gracious to me and patient with me throughout the healing process. I believe His heart was grieved over the situation, watching one child of God belittle another. In contrast to the words this person spoke to tear down, God spoke His Word of life to my heart, overflowing with love and comfort and grace, which built up, encouraged, and brought healing.

God has made us part of His family; we are the body of Christ! Not only for the furtherance of His kingdom but as a support system for one another. We need to pray for discernment and sensitivity when dealing with others. We need to be intentional about showing the grace and compassion of Christ in our interactions and relationships, meeting people where they are. Our lives should be such that our words and actions draw others to Jesus where they can find healing and grow in grace, contributing to the body of Christ and its health. 1 Corinthians 12:26 tells us if one part of the body suffers, every part suffers with it. And if one part is honored, every part rejoices with it. Therefore, our hurtful words and actions don't only do harm to the person(s) to whom they were directed. There are ripple effects that cause damage to the entire body. Likewise, when we support and encourage one another in Christ, we rejoice together as we see one another grow and be further conformed into the image of Jesus.

The Bible says that the world will know that we are Jesus's disciples because of the love we have for one another (John 13:35). Jesus tells us to let our light shine before others that they may see our good works and glorify God (Matt. 5:16). Paul pleads with us to "be completely humble and gentle; be patient, bearing with one another in love. Make every effort to keep the unity of the Spirit through the bond of peace" (Eph. 4:2–3 [NIV]). As followers of Christ, we are the salt of the earth and the light of the world (Matt. 5:13–14). We are ambassadors for Christ! (2 Cor. 5:20). Every day in our homes, workplaces, communities, churches, and everywhere in between, we are representing Christ. We are His image bearers, created to reflect His character. David, whom the Bible refers to as a man after God's own heart, stated that it was God's gentleness that made him great (Ps. 18:35). In the book of Philippians, Paul exhorts us to let our gentleness be evident to all (4:5–7). And Peter tells us to love each other deeply because love covers a multitude of sins (1 Pet. 4:8). Sisters, wave high God's banner of love to the world around you. It is His love that draws us to Him, not His judgment.

18

Forgiveness: Part 1

Matthew 26:28 (ESV)
This is my blood of the covenant, which is poured
out for many for the forgiveness of sins.

Forgiveness ... it's a difficult topic. So many opinions. So many perspectives. And, as I've said before, I am no theologian or scholar. But one thing I hope we can all agree on is that it's not optional. It may not always come immediately, but it is the place we all need to come to when someone has hurt us or sinned against us.

To start, I think it would be helpful to remember that not all sin is deliberate. Even Jesus, while hanging on the cross, said, "Father, forgive them, for they do not know what they are doing" (Luke 23:34). It is possible for someone to speak or behave in a way that is hurtful without them realizing it, without there being intent. They may be clueless, or they may truly believe that what they are saying or doing is right. I guarantee each one of us is guilty of doing the very same thing and will likely be guilty of it again in the future. While we can sometimes become defensive when we are told that we've offended or hurt another, I think, for the most part, we are genuinely sorry and seek their forgiveness. How hurt would you be if they assumed ill intent, marred your character to others, and were unwilling to forgive you? Ladies, let it never be said of us! We must be able to have mature conversations with one another as problems and conflicts arise and give others the benefit of the doubt.

Things become a little trickier when there is a pattern of sin, a lifestyle of sin. When we have people in our life that are not saved, which we all do, this is going to be an ongoing issue. Chances are they are not going to feel remorseful, even if confronted in love, but justified, maybe even indignant that you would suggest any wrongdoing on their part. Dealing with this kind of person is hard, and sometimes boundaries need to be put in place. However, we still need to honor God by obeying His Word that tells us to forgive. You never know when your decision to forgive and extend God's grace toward an unsaved person may lead them to a personal relationship with Jesus Christ where their sins can be ultimately forgiven.

Let's face it: being sinned against is going to be a problem with believers as well because we are all selfish and sinful by nature. Being sinned against by another believer can be some of the most painful wrongs done to us because we expect the person to know better. We expect more of that person as a fellow follower of Christ. Clearly, our lives should no longer be characterized by sin. We should be seeking daily to obey God's Word and walk in His ways. However, none of us will be without sin until we are united with Christ in His kingdom. Remember: each of us is at a different place in our walk with the Lord and at a different maturity level in our relationship with Him. While that is not an excuse for sin, some of us may be a little rougher around the edges than others. Let's continue to have grace for one another, acknowledging our own sin and continual need of forgiveness before bringing down the hammer on someone for their sin.

Then there's willful and deliberate sin. There are countless men, women, and children who have experienced horrors at the hands of others and their sinfulness: children abused by a parent or family member, physically, sexually, mentally, or emotionally; marriages and families broken and shattered through domestic violence; a spouse who betrays the other through an act(s) of adultery; sibling rivalries and jealousies that run so deep, your interactions with them could be likened to that of an enemy instead of your very own flesh and blood. What does forgiveness look like in these situations? Well, I can tell you what forgiveness does not look like.

Forgiveness does not mean that you are a doormat to be walked over and trampled on day in and day out. You are a child of the Most High God, created in His image, washed in His blood, heir to His kingdom, and valued as priceless. Being someone who extends forgiveness does not give people license to manipulate or take advantage of you while you sit there defenseless. We are by no means defenseless! "God is our refuge and strength, an ever-present help in trouble" (Ps. 46:1 [NIV]).

Forgiveness does not always mean that things can go back to the way they were—it does not always mean restoration of a relationship. However, our willingness to forgive someone who has hurt us takes away that persons' power over us. God's desire for us to forgive those who sin against us is not only out of obedience to His Word but for our health and benefit as well.

Last, forgiveness does not mean forgetting. It does not mean that we forget what happened or that the memory of it will never sting and cause pain or sadness. On the other hand, we should not be holding someone's sin over their head and continually reminding them of it. If this is happening, it could be an indicator that maybe you have not yet truly forgiven them. While forgiveness is a choice, it is not always an easy one. Some hurts cut so deep and have bled for so long that it feels they could take the very life of us if we do not guard those wounds from being touched. Forgiveness can feel like a threat, one that will remove the protections put in place, leaving you vulnerable. If you find yourself struggling to come to a place of forgiveness in your heart toward someone, go to God and confess your struggle. "For we do not have a high priest who is unable to empathize with our weaknesses, but we have one who has been tempted in every way, just as we are yet he did not sin. Let us then approach God's throne of grace with confidence, so that we may receive mercy and find grace to help us in our time of need" (Heb. 4:15–16 [NIV]).

19

Forgiveness: Part 2

Proverbs 13:10 (NIV)
Where there is strife, there is pride, but wisdom
is found in those who take advice.

Ecclesiastes 7:8 (ESV)
The end of a thing is better than its beginning; The
patient in spirit is better than the proud in spirit.

Last week, I touched on the effect other people's sin has on our life and our need to come to a place of forgiveness toward them as Jesus taught us. This week, the tables are turned, and I will be talking about our need to seek the forgiveness of others when we are the ones who have sinned against them.

Why is it that we, as a people, so often find it difficult to admit wrongdoing? furthermore, to acknowledge our flat-out sin against another person? Why does this chide against us so? Have you ever felt like asking someone's forgiveness was so difficult that you felt a physical strain on your heart? Have you ever felt like the words "please forgive me" were such a lump in your throat that you were nearly choking to get them out? Have you ever gotten those words out of your mouth only to be followed quickly by "But …" as you fill in the blank with the justification for what you said or did? All of this is our pride rearing its ugly head. It is a human condition. We all struggle with it to one degree or another. And the sooner we recognize it and acknowledge it for what it is, the sooner we can work on uprooting it from our hearts.

As we see from our scripture references this week, the Bible has something to say about the issue of pride. There are many more references throughout scripture than those I listed. What that tells us is that it is an epidemic that has run rampant throughout the entirety of human history. In fact, it started even before we were created. The first reference to pride is that of Satan when he was cast out of heaven and down to earth for saying in his heart that he would ascend to the heavens, exalt his throne above Almighty God's, and make himself like the Most High (Isa. 14:12–14). Regardless, scripture also tells us that pride has no place among God's people, no matter what shape or form it takes.

If we are regularly confessing our sins to the Lord, then we should be keenly aware of how daily we need God's forgiveness. We need to become as cognizant of our sins against others and be comfortable confessing them to the person(s) affected and asking their forgiveness. James, the brother of Jesus, tells us to confess our sins to each other and pray for each other (James 5:16). Forgiveness is foundational in any relationship. Every strong marriage and friendship I have known has been one abundant in grace for one another's failings and quick to seek forgiveness from each other when hurts are inflicted. If you think there's even a possibility that you may have offended someone, even unintentionally, go to that person and ask their forgiveness. If you feel you have both sinned against one another and you're waiting for the other person to ask first, don't! Be the bigger person and do what you know is right. Take responsibility for your part in the problem. Those three words, "Please forgive me," have incredible power to heal and restore. Don't be afraid to say them often. The health of your relationships depends on it.

20

Forgiveness: Part 3

2 Corinthians 11:3 (ESV)
But I am afraid that as the serpent deceived Eve
by his cunning, your thoughts will be led astray
from a sincere and pure devotion to Christ.

I want to spend one more week on the topic of forgiveness. I've already addressed both the need to forgive others and the need to ask forgiveness of others. This week, I want to discuss the grace and forgiveness we need for ourselves when we sin or feel we have failed. Being convicted by the Spirit about sin is a good thing. It is a gift from God that reminds us that we belong to Him and shows us when we are living and operating outside of His will for us. It is intended to turn us toward God in repentance where we receive His grace and forgiveness. The problem is His voice is not the only voice vying for our attention. The enemy is also eager to swoop in but with accusations. If we are not prepared, those accusations can drown out the voice of the Holy Spirit in our lives.

The voice of the Spirit directs us to God's Word, where we find His truths and His promises. In contrast, Satan prompts us to question

God and His Word, whispering, "Did God really say ... ?" (Gen. 3:1 [NIV]). One would think discerning between the two voices would be plain and simple, right? At times, it is, but the devil is cunning. He is the father of all lies (John 8:44), and he seeks to deceive the multitudes (Rev. 12:9). He knows our weaknesses, he knows our inclinations, he knows our fears and insecurities, and he knows when to strike and precisely where to hit us. He knows that as children of God, we feel deeply remorseful for our sin; therefore, he will do whatever it takes to keep us stuck in a cycle of guilt and shame. He would have us convinced that we cannot go to God for forgiveness again. Not this time ... We have gone too far. We sin too often. We have asked too many times. We have broken too many promises. We are too much. We are not enough. We know better. We are not worthy of His forgiveness. Satan would have us believe that we are the exception to God's Word—that the blood of Jesus is not sufficient for our sin, only for others. Why is it sometimes so easy to believe him? Because too often they are things we already believe about ourselves. Whether it's what our families communicated to us past and present, what our friends show us by their actions, what the world says about us through social media, what our insecurities have been telling us for years, or all of the above. To one degree or another, we have bought into the lie that God's love is not unconditional, at least not for us.

First and foremost, we must recognize these accusations for what they are: *lies*. Satan will do whatever he can to draw you away from God and render you ineffective for the furtherance of His kingdom. There is constant spiritual warfare, and the battlefield is often the mind. This is one reason why we are told to be transformed by the renewing of our minds (Rom. 12:2). This is not a once-and-done event in our lives. We must do it regularly and repeatedly throughout our days and our lives by reading the Word of God and applying it. I have a friend who shared that anytime she feels bombarded by accusations, she prays through the scriptures, reminding herself of

God's promises. This is how she actively renews her mind with God's truth. What better thing could you do, especially in those moments, than recognize the lie, refute it, and stand on the promises of God's Word? The truth is you are covered in the precious blood of Christ. That is what God sees when He looks at you. He sees Jesus's blood and His perfect sacrifice on your behalf. Nothing more and nothing less. There is nothing that can separate you from the love of God that is in Christ Jesus (Rom. 8).

Upon research, I found that there are 5,467 divine promises in the Word of God. I don't know about you, but I am still trying to wrap my head around that number. We have got some major studying to do, ladies! But, in the meantime, I selected a few to encourage you.

> Hebrews 8:12 (ESV)
> For I will be merciful toward their iniquities, and I will remember their sins no more.

> Isaiah 43:25 (NLT)
> I—yes, I alone—will blot out your sins for my own sake and will never think of them again.

> Psalm 103:10–14 (NLT)
> He does not punish us for all our sins; he does not deal harshly with us, as we deserve. For his unfailing love toward those who fear him is as great as the height of the heavens above the earth. He has removed our sins as far from us as the east is from the west. The LORD is like a father to his children, tender and compassionate to those who fear him. For he knows how weak we are; he remembers we are only dust.

I hope you will find rest and comfort in these promises.

21

Sacrificial Love

Isaiah 53:4–5 (NIV)

Surely he took up our pain and bore our suffering …
He was pierced for our transgressions, he was crushed
for our iniquities; the punishment that brought us peace
was on him, and by his wounds we are healed.

Hebrews 2:10–13 (NIV)

In bringing many sons and daughters to glory, it was fitting
that God, for whom and through whom everything exists,
should make the pioneer of their salvation perfect through
what he suffered. Both the one who makes people holy
and those who are made holy are of the same family. So,
Jesus is not ashamed to call them brothers and sisters.
He says, "I will declare your name to my brothers and
sisters; in the assembly I will sing your praises." And
again, "I will put my trust in him." And again, he says,
"Here am I, and the children God has given me."

Are there passages of scripture that are challenging? Yes. Are
there passages that convict us about our words, actions, and thought

life? Yes. Are there passages that, if we're honest, our sinful nature wishes were not in there? Yes. But, above all, the Bible displays God's unconditional love, incomprehensible grace, and unimaginable sacrifice of Jesus for us and our sins, past, present, and future. He saw them all and died for us still so we could be washed, cleansed, and forgiven; so we could be restored to the Father; so we could know the riches of His grace and His love for us; so we could know and fulfill the purpose for which He created us through the power of His Spirit. All of this because He wants us. He doesn't need us in any way, shape, or form. But He wants us. He wants us to know Him, to walk with Him in our daily lives, and to be with Him for all eternity.

Why? I will never truly know. I will never comprehend why He would want anything to do with someone like me. But He does. And He has made the ultimate sacrifice to prove it. Hearing Jesus cry out, "My God, My God, why have You forsaken Me," as He hung on the cross, the Father turned His face away from His cries. If He didn't, I never could have been saved. I cannot hold back the tears as I type this. Such a love is incomprehensible—the Father willing to turn His face away and the Son willing to make the ultimate sacrifice, not for any sin of His own but for mine, so I could be forgiven, redeemed, and renewed. One of my most beloved verses in the Bible is Isaiah 49:15–16: "Can a mother forget the baby at her breast and have no compassion on the child she has borne? Though she may forget, I will not forget you! See, I have engraved you on the palms of my hands" (NIV).

Long before I was born, my name was already engraved on the palms of His hands; your name was engraved on the palms of His hands. He loved us even before the foundation of the world (Eph. 1:4). All the days ordained for us were written in His book before even one of them came to be (Ps. 139:16). He knows all of our sorrows and our wanderings, collects our tears in His bottle, and records each one of them in His book (Ps. 56:8). When I stop and think about these things, I echo David's declaration in Psalm 139, "Such knowledge is too wonderful for me, too great for me to understand" (v. 6 [NLT]).

22

The Gift of Prayer

James 5:16 (AMP)
Therefore, confess your sins to one another [your false
steps, your offenses], and pray for one another, that you
may be healed and restored. The heartfelt and persistent
prayer of a righteous man (believer) is able to accomplish
much [when put into action and made effective by
God—it is dynamic and can have tremendous power].

Romans 12:12 (NIV)
Be joyful in hope, patient in affliction, faithful in prayer.

There are some who believe or who have been taught and made
to feel that asking for prayer is a sign of weakness. On the contrary,
it is a sign of strength and wisdom when you recognize that you
cannot do everything on your own—that you are dependent upon
God and His strength, wisdom, and guidance. It means you have a
humble heart, which is precious in God's sight. If Jesus felt the need
to get alone before the Father and pray, as well as taking time to pray

with others, then, surely, we should be doing the same. Below are a few of many examples of the importance of prayer.

As we see in James 5:16 above, prayer is both powerful and effective and can accomplish incredible things in our lives and the lives of others. It is a privilege to pray for one another, and we should seek the Holy Spirit's help in reminding us to pray regularly for those who ask us and for those whom we know are in need. In addition, prayer, along with the Word of God, is the most powerful weapon we have against the enemy. "The weapons we fight with are not the weapons of the world. On the contrary, they have divine power to demolish strongholds" (2 Cor. 10:4 [NIV]). Not only does prayer defend us from Satan and his attacks, but also it can shield us from making decisions that are outside of God's will for us and, therefore, potentially harmful to us.

Prayer is also an act of worship. We are acknowledging that He alone is God when we come before Him in the name of Jesus and bring our petitions. This, in and of itself, glorifies God. However, in addition to our requests, let's be intentional each day about spending time worshipping God for who He is and for all that He has done. I know there are days when we feel anything but worshipful. Maybe the days, weeks, or months have been long and arduous. If we're honest, thankfulness is not exactly overflowing. Maybe even the thought of it is daunting, and bringing ourselves to a place of worship in our hearts seems nearly impossible. It is then that we need to be all the more intentional. "Let us offer through Jesus a continual sacrifice of praise to God, proclaiming our allegiance to his name" (Heb. 13:15 [NLT]).

I realize these examples may seem like the simplest of things—things we all know. But I think sometimes it is the simplest things that so easily get brushed aside or passed over for those that are seemingly more important or pressing. I believe it is in simple acts of faith and prayer that lives are changed and battles are won. Therefore, I want to encourage you all to press on in prayer! Make it a priority, at all times, and in all things. "For you shall eat the fruit of [the labor of] your hands, you will be happy and blessed and it will be well with you" (Ps. 128:2 [AMP]).

23

Unfailing Love

Psalm 143:8 (NIV)
Let the morning bring me word of your unfailing
love, for I have put my trust in you. Show me the
way I should go, for to you I entrust my life.

In the process of writing these devotions, I came across this verse
in my daily reading. I knew I wanted to use this verse as a foundation
for one of my devotions, but, at that moment, I didn't quite know
how I wanted to elaborate on it. Therefore, I typed the verse on a
blank document, clicked Save, and decided I'd come back to it at a
later time. Now, months later, during a time of prayer and fasting,
the Lord brought it to my attention that I had not gotten back to it
and it was time. So I set out to work on it the following day; that day
being today. I sat down this morning to have my devotion, prayer,
and Bible reading time, and my devotion's verse for today was Psalm
90:14: "Satisfy us in the morning with Your unfailing love, that
we may sing for joy and be glad all our days" (NIV). Then, after a
time of prayer, I flipped to today's scripture on my little calendar
in the kitchen and read the following verse: "Surely Your goodness
and unfailing love will pursue me all the days of my life, and I will

live in the house of the LORD forever" (Ps. 23:6 [NLT]). Then I proceeded to sit down at the computer to write this devotion, and there it was … a blank page with nothing but our verse for today listed above: "Let the morning bring me word of Your unfailing love, for I have put my trust in You. Show me the way I should go, for to You I entrust my life" (Ps. 143:8 [NIV]).

It was then that the Lord spoke to my heart, saying, "This is the message I want you to share today—My unfailing love." I stopped for a moment, in awe of how He orchestrated all of this. He knew that I would be reading the first two scriptures during my time with Him this morning and made it a point to reveal to me last night that I had forgotten to go back and work on this devotion whose foundation was our verse for today. Only He could have aligned all three of those verses today to impress upon me the depth of His never-ending and unfailing love, furthermore, prompting me to share it with all of you. Clearly, this must be something many of us need to be reminded of in this season of life. Are you struggling with a sense of failure? His love for you is unfailing! Struggling with disappointment? His love for you is unfailing! Struggling with fear and doubt? His love for you is unfailing! Feeling overcome with regret? His love for you is unfailing! Are you feeling overwhelmed by a sense of hopelessness? His love for you is unfailing!

Determine in your hearts today, whatever your circumstances, you are going to entrust your life to Him because He is trustworthy. Determine in your hearts today that no matter how dark, how helpless, or how hopeless you feel that you will sing for joy because God is good and He is worthy of your praise. Determine in your hearts today to live in light of eternity, fixing your eyes not on things that are seen but on those that are unseen because of His promise that you will live in the house of the Lord forever (2 Cor. 4:18, Ps. 23:6). Seek Him every morning, before your day begins, and ask Him to satisfy you with is unfailing love—to remind you that His goodness will follow you all the days of your life and to show you the way you should go as you place your heart and your life into the palm of His hands every day, trusting and surrendering to His good and perfect will.

Rest in His love for you this week, my friends, his unchangeable, unfailing love for you.

24

Relentless Pursuit

Hebrews 13:8 (NIV)
Jesus Christ is the same yesterday and today and forever.

The past seven years have been challenging for me. They have been some of the hardest years of my life. There are times I have felt as if I was drowning in doubt and confusion to the point of feeling that if I continued down this path, I would lose my mind. As a result, there have been times I have shut down and shut God out in many ways, keeping Him at arm's length. In my heart, I was hiding, running, guarding, and protecting—so fearful to let Him into my life as I once did.

But no matter what I did, He continually pursued me. No matter how far I ran, how well I tried to hide, no matter how angry I became, and, if I am honest, how disrespectful I was toward Him, He remained. He pursued me still. He refused to leave me in such a place of darkness and chaos. He refused to leave me alone even when, at times, that's what I thought I wanted Him to do.

But His love for me is too great. His faithfulness to His promises too binding. He would not, could not leave me, His blood-bought child, His beloved. And I think that is one of the most important things He wanted me to learn in all of this—that truly nothing can separate me from the love of God that is in Christ Jesus. He wanted me to know the depths of His faithfulness, love, and provision for me. Truly, they are unending. They are unconditional. He loves me because of who He is, not because of anything I have done.

25

Faith and Obedience

1 Kings 8:56 (NLT)
Praise the LORD who has given rest to his people Israel, just as he promised. Not one word has failed of all the wonderful promises he gave through his servant Moses.

Joshua 23:14 (NLT)
Deep in your hearts you know that every promise of the LORD your God has come true. Not a single one has failed.

God's Word is the only truth upon which anyone can stand. God's promises are the only ones that will never fail. Throughout the Old Testament, we see God giving promise after promise to His people. Nevertheless, they needed to have faith that He was able to carry out His plans and walk in obedience to His direction so that they would see His promises fulfilled.

God led the Israelites out of Egypt and through the Red Sea so they could lay claim to the land that God had promised them. However, this would be no easy task. God's promise was sure, but the Israelites would face many enemies and fight many battles along the way to seeing God's promise come to fruition. Not long after the miracle of crossing the Red Sea, the Israelites were confronted by warriors of that land. Instead of succumbing to fear of the enemy, Moses trusted God to bring them into the Promised Land as He foretold and went to war. That battle was won and many thereafter. Word about God, His power, and His protection over His people spread throughout the surrounding nations. The people's faith in God and His promises and their willingness to let their faith lead them to action brought not only victory for them but also glory and honor to God. Their obedience was a testament to God's faithfulness and His ability to move mightily on behalf of His people.

Since God is the same yesterday, today, and forever (Heb. 13:8), we can be confident that our faith, testimony, and witness for Christ can also have a profound impact on others, especially our families and friends, as well as any other circle of influence the Lord has given you, even if it is not always evident.

I pray God continues to strengthen you, emboldening you to be a resounding testament of His love and His faithfulness to the world around you. I pray that He fills you afresh with His Spirit—that out of you would flow rivers of His living water, leading many into the presence of our Savior (John 7:38).

26

Hurt and the Healer

Romans 8:39 (NIV)
Neither height nor depth, nor anything else in
all creation, will be able to separate us from
the love of God that is in Christ Jesus.

Living in a fallen world, brokenness is something we all experience throughout our lives. However, some wounds are so deep, so permeating, so crippling that we can feel broken beyond repair. The scars that they have left are too large to completely hide. Our woundedness infiltrates our thoughts, words, and relationships, like a hostile enemy who secretly and gradually moves throughout each area of our lives, seeking to claim territory and rule over it.

We can become weary of the struggle to overcome, feeling overwhelmed and defeated. We cry out to God, press into Jesus through prayer, and surrender to Him the best we know how, casting our burdens upon Him. Yet there are days where the pain seeks to undo us, times when hope eludes us. Proverbs tells us that "hope deferred makes the heart sick" (13:12 [NKJV]). I am all too familiar with this heart sickness, earnestly longing for the latter part of verse 12, which states, "But a desire given is a tree of life."

In the waiting and the trusting, we may falter and fail. Yet I know there is no height or depth, width, or length that He's unwilling to go to heal our hearts and minds and to restore the years the locusts have eaten (Eph. 3:18–19, Joel 2:25).

27

Vulnerability

Isaiah 58:11 (NKJV)
The LORD will guide you continually, and satisfy
your soul in drought, and strengthen your bones;
You shall be like a watered garden, and like a
spring of water, whose waters do not fail.

Have you ever felt like a fraud? A friend of mine and I discussed this once. She shared that she often feels like a fraud, not because she's living a double life or reveling in sin when no one is watching and pretending to be a "good" Christian when someone is; only that if other people really knew her—her flaws, failures, doubts, struggles, fears, and so forth—they wouldn't like her. Therefore, because God does know her inside and out that He must not like her.

I can relate to feeling like a fraud. If I'm honest, I have often felt the same. In fact, in a recent email, this friend said to me, "I respect your strength." I thought to myself, *Me, strong? No …* At that moment, I felt like a fraud. I thought to myself, *I hope I haven't painted a picture of someone I'm not,* and proceeded to share with her what I am about to share with you.

Ladies, every word I have spoken to you through these devotions has been from my heart, and everything I have shared with you has been true. But, to be honest, I struggle with anxiety, fear, and depression more often than I would like to admit. I also struggle with perfectionism, especially when it comes to my relationship with God, and wrestle with deep-seated feelings of consistently disappointing Him. Such things make me feel like a failure to God and everyone around me; the weight of which can be crushing. In the midst of it all, the enemy whispers, "There is no help for you in God" (Ps. 3:2).

But then a passage of scripture from the book of John comes to mind that says,

> From this time many of his disciples turned back and no longer followed him. "You do not want to leave too, do you?" Jesus asked the Twelve. Simon Peter answered him, "Lord, to whom shall we go? You have the words of eternal life. We have come to believe and to know that you are the Holy One of God" (John 6:66–69 [NIV]).

This is what it all boils down to. No matter what I'm feeling, no matter what I'm going through, no matter how insurmountable things may seem, I know with all of my heart, at my very core, that Jesus is the only way, the only truth, and the only life. To whom else would I go? Whom else or what else could I run to that could offer me anything worthwhile and lasting? No one and nothing. Jesus alone can satisfy. He alone can heal. He alone gives life. And there is no hope for me outside of Him. The same is true for you—for us all.

God sees you, all of you, and loves you anyway. He sees you, knows you, and loves you still. He has not and will not ever reject you. He is gracious and merciful. He knows our weaknesses and remembers that we are dust (Ps. 103:14). His compassions never fail. Great is His faithfulness (Lam. 3:22) even when our faithfulness is not.

28

New Creation

2 Corinthians 5:17 (NLT)
This means that anyone who belongs to Christ has become
a new person. The old life is gone; a new life has begun.

As followers of Christ, we know the beauty and the freedom of a
life redeemed, forgiven, and full of the unconditional love of our great
God. But we also know the pain and rejection that sometimes comes
from those who do not understand or accept the new life we've been
given when we receive Jesus as Lord and Savior. Our families may
now mock, judge, or ridicule us for living our lives according to God's
Word instead of the ways of the world. Those who once called us friend
may now reject us for putting God first in our lives and His will for us
instead of their wants and expectations of us.

I have one such instance that stands out for me. I had a coworker
once whom I connected with almost instantly. It didn't take long
before she and I became friends and started spending time together
outside of work. I thought we were good friends until one particular
day. At the time we were friends, I still drank alcohol. So, sometimes,
we would go out and have a couple of drinks, or we would go to

happy hours in the evening after work and sometimes social events on the weekends that always included alcohol. However, one day, while I was reading the Word and praying, the Lord made it very clear that this was not something that He wanted in my life anymore. The alcohol had to go. It was a sobering moment (no pun intended).

I was reading about the Second Coming of Christ and the Rapture in Matthew 24. It spoke of how no one knows when Jesus will return for us but that we are to watch and be ready! It speaks about those who say to themselves, "God won't be back for a while, I've got time to get it together," and continue living the way they want to, partying, getting drunk, and so forth, and how that mindset is futile and has consequences. I remember thinking to myself, *What if Jesus returned for me and I was drunk? What would I do if He was standing before me? How could I look Him in the face?* The thought of it was unbearable. It cut me to the core. I knew with all of my heart that God was telling me that alcohol no longer had a place in my life. I immediately repented, asked His forgiveness, and determined to live my life according to His will in every area and not my own. Not that I have done that perfectly by any means, but it remains the desire of my heart.

I knew that difficult conversations with family and friends were going to follow. I recall the day when I told this friend that I believed this was something that I needed to put down. Her response was less than supportive. She flat out said she did not accept this "new me." I assured her that I was the same old me minus the two of us going out for drinks, but she just wouldn't accept it. Sadly, that was the end of our friendship. But I guess we were never really friends if alcohol and partying were the only glue that kept us together.

Walking with Christ is not always the easiest road. In fact, God's Word says the road that leads to life is narrow and at times hard, with few willing to traverse such a path. Therefore, there are not many who find it. But wide is the road, and easy to travel is the path that leads to destruction; many choosing ease and comfort over truth and righteousness. Therefore, many are they that enter that path (Matt. 7:13–14). But those who follow the narrow way know that while at times it is difficult, it is the only path to true life, to a life filled with purpose, meaning, and extraordinary promises and riches that are ours in Christ Jesus. It is the only road that leads to heaven—to eternity in God's kingdom. It is where we find hope that sees us through the struggles and heartache that this world so often brings and the blessed assurance that leads us face-to-face with our Savior, where we will be embraced by Him and hear those words we all long to hear: "Well done, my good and faithful servant" (Matt. 25:21 [NLT]).

There is nothing on earth worth holding on to that is worth forfeiting the promises of God and the glory that has yet to come. Paul tells us that all the things that made him important and acceptable in the world's eyes: confidence in his good works and his own effort to accomplish things, his ethnicity, his upbringing, his prominent position as a religious figure, a respected leader among his people, his zeal in following the law perfectly; all things that were considered to be of worth and importance, he considered worthless once he knew Christ personally and all that He had done on his behalf. In Philippians 3:7–8, Paul tells us, "I once thought these things were valuable, but now I consider them worthless because of what Christ has done. Yes, everything else is worthless when compared with the infinite value of knowing Christ Jesus my Lord" (NLT).

As we see in our verse for this week's devotion, when we receive Christ as Lord and Savior, we are given a new life. In that moment, a new life begins, and the old life—our old ways of thinking, living, and interacting with others—start to change as we are conformed more and more into the image and likeness of Jesus. We are no longer slaves to our sinful nature and its desires. However, those who have not made the decision to receive Christ, and therefore are not indwelt with the Holy Spirit, don't understand the changes that continually take place in our lives as we grow in the knowledge of God and in our relationship with Him. And they never will unless they also acknowledge their sin, accept Christ as Lord and Savior of their lives, and receive His forgiveness. Therefore, there are always going to be some who reject us, and, as we all know, rejection can be quite painful, especially when it comes at the hands of those we love.

But I want to encourage you despite the heartbreak that may come to hold on to Jesus with everything in you! Do not allow such things to take away from your faith in Christ. Jesus understands rejection and betrayal more deeply than we will ever know. He is ready and waiting to help you in your time of need and to heal the wounds that are inflicted upon you in this fallen world. I pray you will sit with the scriptures I have listed below and ask God to speak to your heart personally—to strengthen you according to His Word for whatever challenges you may be facing presently or to prepare you for those that will one day come.

Hebrews 4:14–16 (NIV)
Therefore, since we have a great high priest who has ascended into heaven, Jesus the Son of God, let us hold firmly to the faith we profess. For we do not have a high priest who is unable to empathize with our weaknesses, but we have one who has been tempted in every way, just as we are—yet he did not sin. Let us then approach God's throne of grace with confidence, so that we may receive mercy and find grace to help us in our time of need.

1 Peter 1:6–7 (NLT)
So be truly glad. There is wonderful joy ahead, even though you must endure many trials for a

little while. These trials will show that your faith is genuine. It is being tested as fire tests and purifies gold—though your faith is far more precious than gold. So when your faith remains strong through many trials, it will bring you much praise and glory and honor on the day when Jesus Christ is revealed to the whole world.

Hebrews 10:35 (AMP)
Do not throw away your [fearless] confidence, for it has a glorious and great reward. For you have need of patient endurance [to bear up under difficult circumstances without compromising], so that when you have done the will of God, you may receive and enjoy to the full what is promised.

29

God's Faithfulness

Lamentations 3:22–24 (AMP)
It is because of the LORD's lovingkindnesses that we
are not consumed, because His [tender] compassions
never fail. They are new every morning; Great and
beyond all measure is Your faithfulness. "The LORD is
my portion and my inheritance," says my soul; "Therefore
I have hope in Him and wait expectantly for Him."

I read a devotion that quoted part of the song "Great Is Thy
Faithfulness," and my eyes filled with tears. Each word filled my
heart with peace, comfort, and contentment, for I know the words
to be true in the deepest parts of my being through a personal
relationship with Jesus, my Savior, although this relationship has
not always been easy.

There are some whose life experiences I know well. Others I have
walked side by side with during difficult times. Still others I know
very little, if anything at all. But one thing I know for sure is that
pain and suffering touch us all; some less, some more, but there is
not one life that escapes its sting. As a result, I know it can be hard at

times to view God and your relationship with Him in a positive way. I know it can be difficult to see Him as a God of love, compassion, and understanding. I know it can be hard to trust Him—hard to believe the good things He says about you in His word and feels toward you in His heart. But, this week, I want to remind you of His unfailing, unconditional love for you. His compassion, mercy, and grace are immeasurable. They are all for you, the one He loves. These aren't just words; they are truths. They are part of God's very own character. They cannot be separated from who He is. It is what He says about Himself in His Word, and "God is not a man that He should lie" (Num. 23:19 [NKJV]).

I hope and pray that as you continue to seek Him and know Him more, He will enable you to see yourself through His eyes, that you will know with all your heart, through personal experience in your relationship with Him, that you are indeed the one He loves, the one whom He deemed worth dying to save, the one whom He desires to have a unique and personal relationship, different from what He has with anyone else in all of His creation. His purpose and calling on your life are just as unique. Trust Him with your heart. Place it in His hands each day. He will heal you, and He will restore you. Trust Him to do it. He is trustworthy.

> Pardon for sin and a peace that endureth,
> Thine own dear presence to cheer and to guide;
> Strength for today and bright hope for tomorrow,
> Blessings all mine, with ten thousand beside!
> "Great is Thy faithfulness!"
> "Great is Thy faithfulness!"
> Morning by morning new mercies I see;
> All I have needed Thy hand hath provided—
> "Great is Thy faithfulness," Lord, unto me!
> ("Great Is Thy Faithfulness" by Thomas Obediah Chisholm)

30

Strength

Ephesians 3:16–21 (NIV)

I pray that out of his glorious riches he may strengthen you
with power through his Spirit in your inner being, so that
Christ may dwell in your hearts through faith. And I pray
that you, being rooted and established in love, may have
power, together with all the Lord's holy people, to grasp
how wide and long and high and deep is the love of Christ,
and to know this love that surpasses knowledge—that you
may be filled to the measure of all the fullness of God.
Now to him who is able to do immeasurably more than all
we ask or imagine, according to his power that is at work
within us, to him be glory in the church and in Christ Jesus
throughout all generations, for ever and ever! Amen.

Matthew 11:28–29 (NLT)

Then Jesus said, "Come to me, all of you who are weary
and carry heavy burdens, and I will give you rest. Take my
yoke upon you. Let me teach you, because I am humble
and gentle at heart, and you will find rest for your souls."

1 Chronicles 16:11 (NIV)
Look to the LORD and his strength; seek his face always.

I have a friend who shared her broken heart with me over the news that her son, daughter-in-law, and grandchildren would be moving out of state to start a new job. The news of a new position was welcome, but the news of their departure was like a dagger in her heart. The reality of her beloved son, his wife, and her precious grandchildren no longer being a part of her everyday life was a major blow that knocked the wind right out of her. The sense of loss she felt was palpable. She expressed her hurt, feelings of overwhelm, and a desire to be stronger while processing the brokenness she felt over the many losses she has had over the last year. She ended our conversation asking for prayer that this time would be used for God to become bigger in her life, acknowledging that He alone could fill the void she was feeling.

This conversation led me to consider the meaning of strength. Our society says we should be strong, especially as women. But what does it mean to be strong? Whose definition of strength do we live by? the world's view that says we shouldn't allow anything or anyone to hurt us? that everything should just roll off our backs? that when we share our feelings, we're really just complaining and need to suck it up and move on?

A hurting heart, doubts, fears, and the like are not signs of weakness or a lack of strength. They are part of being human. Are they things we should bring before the Lord in prayer? Yes! Are they things He can enable us to overcome? Absolutely! But they are not wrong in and of themselves, nor should anyone make you feel ashamed for wrestling with such things, including yourself. Sometimes, the same grace and understanding we would wholeheartedly extend to someone else in a difficult place, we need to learn to give ourselves.

In 2 Corinthians 12:9–10, we read, "But He has said to me, 'My grace is sufficient for you [My lovingkindness and My mercy are more than enough—always available—regardless of the situation]; for [My] power is being perfected [and is completed and shows itself most effectively] in [your] weakness.' Therefore, I will all the more gladly boast in my weaknesses, so that the power of Christ [may completely enfold me and] may dwell in me ... for when I am weak [in human strength], then I am strong [truly able, truly powerful, truly drawing from God's strength]" (AMP).

As followers of Christ, this needs to be the definition of strength we live by. This friend, despite the hurt she was feeling, wanted God to have a greater place in her life in the midst of her pain and recognized that He alone can heal—that He alone can fulfill us. I'd say that is an amazing response to a broken heart and most certainly a sign of strength—a strength that is precious in the sight of God and to the heart of God.

31

Loss: Part 1

1 Peter 1:3 (NIV)
Praise be to the God and Father of our Lord Jesus Christ! In his great mercy he has given us new birth into a living hope through the resurrection of Jesus Christ from the dead.

Loss ... a word all of us dread, maybe even fear, yet one we all know and some of us too well. I think the first thing that comes to mind for many is the loss of people we love. I have three friends who have all lost adult children, two others who have had miscarriages, one of whom has experienced multiple losses. Both of my sisters have lost their fathers. A friend has lost her husband. And I lost my beloved grandfather far too young. I have also lost my best friend, as well as my first love. There is something about the death of those we love that leaves a hole in our hearts. And while God is faithful to bring healing over time, we are never quite the same after such loss.

Yet what we need to remember is our Lord Jesus Christ has overcome death and stands in victory, proclaiming that death does not have the final word! "Death has been swallowed up in victory. Where, O death, is your victory? Where, O death, is your sting? Thanks be to God! He gives us the victory through our Lord Jesus Christ" (1 Cor. 15:54–55, 57). Therefore, when we feel the weight of loss pressing down on us, we can set our hearts and minds on eternity where our heavenly home awaits us (John 3:16) along with those in Christ who have gone before us (1 Thess. 4:13–18 [NIV]). This is our blessed assurance! Therefore, may we all, with endurance, "await and confidently expect the [fulfillment of our] blessed hope and the glorious appearing of our great God and Savior, Christ Jesus" (Titus 2:13 [AMP]).

32

Loss: Part 2

Hebrews 4:16 (NIV)
Let us then approach God's throne of grace with
confidence, so that we may receive mercy and
find grace to help us in our time of need.

Last week, we talked about loss, specifically the loss of loved ones and the eternal hope that we have in Christ. This week, I want to acknowledge that there are many forms of loss that we may experience throughout our lives; all of which can cause sorrow and suffering—for example, loss of a hard-earned career, maybe an unexpected disability or debilitating health condition that changes life as you've known it and steals away the hopes and dreams you had for the future, or maybe an unexpected move out of state that takes away those you love or takes you away from family and friends and the comfort and security they give. These things are a reality for many, and the effects they have on us are just as real.

Sometimes, we never fully come to terms with these varied forms of loss in our lives whether we realize it or not. Consequently, as life continues on, more difficulties arise, and other types of loss are experienced; they can reopen wounds from prior losses that have been suffered. They can also intensify the hurt you feel from those wounds that have never quite healed. If that is you today, I am praying that you would feel God's embrace—that, in some way, He would make His presence known to you, tangible to you; that He would remind you of His love and care for you as His daughter. Those of you who have children know how deep your love is for them. God's love for you is even greater and deeper still. And in His tenderness and gentleness, He promises to bind up the brokenhearted and save those who are crushed in spirit (Ps. 147:3, 34:18).

It is His joy to comfort and care for you. Keep turning to Him. "For You LORD will light my lamp; The LORD my God will enlighten my darkness" (Ps. 18:28 [NKJV]).

33

Time Is Short

1 Peter 1:24–25 (NIV)
All people are like grass, and all their glory is like
the flowers of the field; the grass withers and the
flowers fall, but the word of the Lord endures forever.
And this is the word that was preached to you.

Since we've been discussing the topic of loss the past two
weeks, it felt right to take this week to encourage you to make the
most of whatever time you are given, to take every opportunity God
provides to share the truth of His Word, for we are not promised
tomorrow. Ecclesiastes 9:12 tells us, "No one knows when their hour
will come: As fish are caught in a cruel net, or birds are taken in
a snare, so people are trapped by evil times that fall unexpectedly
upon them" (NIV).

As a nation, we know now more than ever that our entire world, both
personally and collectively, can be turned upside down and inside
out in the blink of an eye. Now, more than ever, we don't know
what a day will bring. Therefore, we must be all the more diligent
and proactive in sharing Christ with those we love who do not yet

know Him. We need to show forth the love of Christ through our words and actions to both those who are saved and those who have not yet given their hearts and lives to Jesus, receiving Him as their Savior and Lord.

2 Corinthians 6:1–2 exhorts us, "As God's partners, we beg you not to accept this marvelous gift of God's kindness and then ignore it. For God says, 'At just the right time, I heard you. On the day of salvation, I helped you.' Indeed, the 'right time' is now. Today is the day of salvation" (NLT). We never know what God is doing in the hearts of others. We never know when our decision to share His Word is going to be exactly what that person needed to step out in faith, believe the truth, and receive God's forgiveness for their sins—to have their names written in the Lamb's book of life and their eternal destination changed forever.

I hope you will join me in praying to the Father and asking for the wisdom, boldness, and sensitivity of the Holy Spirit that we may know how to engage those around us and meet people where they are; that we could say, as Paul did, "I have become all things to all men, so that I may by all means [in any and every way] save some [by leading them to faith in Jesus Christ]. And I do all this for the sake of the gospel, so that I may share in its blessings along with you" (1 Cor. 9:23 [AMP]).

34

Sisters in Christ

Ecclesiastes 4:9–12 (NIV)

Two are better than one, because they have a good return
for their labor: If either of them falls down, one can help
the other up. But pity anyone who falls and has no one
to help them up. Also, if two lie down together, they
will keep warm. But how can one keep warm alone?
Though one may be overpowered, two can defend
themselves. A cord of three strands is not quickly broken.

Today's verse tells us of the importance of having a few close
friends, not just any friends but friends with whom you can lock
arms and walk side by side with throughout life—friends you can
do battle with as we live out our earthly lives in enemy territory.
When we serve together, there is more fruit produced from the
various spiritual gifts and talents that each one contributes. When
one is going through a difficult or painful season of life and finds
themselves faltering or getting knocked down by the trials of life,
the other one is by their side to lift them up and help them bear
their burdens (Gal. 6:2). When Satan is on the prowl and spiritual
warfare ensues, filling our minds with lies and our hearts with doubt

and fear in attempts to take us down, we put on the armor of God together. We stand and fight against his attacks through intercessory prayer and standing on the truth of God's Word together (Eph. 6:10–18).

Ladies, it is of the utmost importance that we have fellow sisters in Christ with whom we can share our life, be encouraged by, and pray with and be prayed for. We each need committed, faithful, and godly friends upon whom we can rely on at all times and in all things. Is this something that you have in your life? How I hope that you do! But if you don't, pray that the Lord would bring one or two others into your life with whom you can have a trusting, fruitful, and godly relationship. God created us for community. We are part of His family. He has made us part of the body of Christ. It is His desire that we have such relationships. Therefore, you can trust Him to answer your prayer and bring the right women into your life at the right time.

I would caution you not to jump ahead of the Lord in this, anxiously seeking someone out. But, instead, prayerfully wait on the Lord to bring along the right person(s). Just because we are all members of His body does not mean that each personality and character is well suited for everyone. The Lord knows you inside and out. He knows your needs, your inclinations, your gifting, and your future. He knows who to bring alongside of you, who will best support and encourage you, both love and challenge you, protect and pray for you, and hold you accountable by speaking the truth in love when needed. It is these types of relationships that enable us to grow "in every way more and more like Christ, who is the head of his body, the church. He makes the whole body fit together perfectly. As each part does its own special work, it helps the other parts grow, so that the whole body is healthy and growing and full of love" (Eph. 4:15–16 [NLT]).

35

Communication

Colossians 4:6 (ESV)
Let your speech always be gracious, seasoned with salt, so
that you may know how you ought to answer each person.

Communication is a topic that I think all of humankind
struggles with throughout every stage of life—husband and wives,
parents and children, teachers and students, friends, and coworkers.
Even the most skilled communicators fall into the trappings of
miscommunication or allow their emotions to get the best of them at
times and say things they should not. Friends, this is an area we need
to give great care and attention to in all our relationships. Otherwise,
the damage that can come as a result of careless or hurtful words
can be irreparable.

The words we choose in communicating with others can make
or break a relationship. They can build someone up or tear them
down. They can heal, or they can harm. They can mend, or they
can shatter. They can praise, or they can curse. It is often when we
are responding emotionally that we get ourselves in trouble. A friend
once said to me that sometimes emotions can be like a caged lion.

What an accurate and vivid description! Unfortunately, the mental picture of letting the lion out of the cage and seeing it tear apart whatever stands before it is just as vivid. I believe this is why the Bible has so much to say about our words and how we should and should not use them. There are far too many scripture references to list here, that's for sure.

However, there is a passage of scripture that I feel sums up many of the others, making God's thoughts on the matter quite clear. Ephesians 4:29, 31–32 reads,

> Do not let unwholesome [foul, profane, worthless, vulgar] words ever come out of your mouth, but only such speech as is good for building up others, according to the need and the occasion, so that it will be a blessing to those who hear [you speak]. Let all bitterness and wrath and anger and clamor [perpetual animosity, resentment, strife, fault-finding] and slander be put away from you, along with every kind of malice [all spitefulness, verbal abuse, malevolence]. Be kind and helpful to one another, tender-hearted [compassionate, understanding], forgiving one another [readily and freely], just as God in Christ also forgave you (AMP).

If God addresses how we use our words this seriously, then we need to also. Luke 6:45 says, "What you say flows from what is in your heart" (NLT). Another translation puts it this way: "Out of the abundance of the heart his mouth speaks" (NKJV). So often we can speak to others and about others from a place of woundedness in our hearts. Therefore, we need to look within ourselves and sit before the Lord, asking Him to reveal the heart issues that are at the root of our communication problems. This is where the work needs to begin. Yet, throughout that process, we must be steadfast in our determination to obey His Word and pray as David did: "Set a guard over my mouth LORD; keep watch over the door of my lips" (Ps. 141:3 [NIV]).

36

Fierce Love

Zephaniah 3:17 (NET)
The LORD your God is in your midst; he is a warrior who can deliver. He takes great delight in you; he renews you by his love; he shouts for joy over you.

Each portion of this verse is a precious promise from our Lord, revealing His heart toward us. First, we read, "The LORD your God is in your midst." This is a promise of His continual presence in the lives of His children. Whether you feel the nearness of God or He feels light-years away, the truth is He is in your midst; He is by your side whether you sense Him or not. Trust the promise of His presence in your life whatever your circumstances. He has promised to never leave you or forsake you (Heb. 13:5).

Second, "He is a warrior who can deliver." God is the warrior of all warriors. He is the only one who is unstoppable, the only one who cannot be conquered. Nothing and no one can stand against our all-powerful God and prevail! No one can thwart His plans and His purposes. You are His daughter, which means you are guarded by His fierce and faithful protection. He will not leave you alone in your struggle with sin. He will not abandon you to the darkness of doubt, confusion, and fear. He will never turn a blind eye to your suffering. He is more than able to deliver us from whatever it is that binds us. Pray to Him for deliverance. Ask and keep on asking! He will bring it about in His perfect timing.

Next, "He takes great delight in you." Really? Me? How can a holy and righteous God see all of me, know all my sins, past, present, and future, and still love me anyway? I will never truly grasp such love. But I know that His Word is inerrant, and, therefore, it is true whether I can understand or perceive it. And when I choose to trust that God takes great delight in me, it brings me incredible joy and rejoicing to the praise of His name!

Furthermore, "He renews you by His love." In 2 Corinthians 5:17, we read, "Therefore, if anyone is in Christ, he is a new creation; old things have passed away; behold, all things have become new" (NKJV). Not only are we renewed by His love through the spiritual rebirth that takes place when we receive Christ as Lord and Savior—a renewal that is permanent and eternal—but He also renews us daily by His love. He is continually conforming us into His image and likeness through His Spirit within us.

Last, "He shouts for joy over you." It is easy for me to look at my life and see all my failures, mistakes, and sins—certainly not a life that would lead a perfect and holy God to shout for joy over me. But what He sees when He looks at me, and at you, is the finished work of Christ on the cross and His blood that covers us, cleanses us, and redeems us. He sees each of our futures and His purposes being fulfilled in and through us. He sees us taking our place in His heavenly kingdom, where He has prepared a home for us, and living for all eternity in the light of His presence. This is what compels Him to shout for joy over us. May these sweet and precious promises bring forth continual shouts of joy from us as well!

37

Refuge

Psalm 28:7 (NIV)
The LORD is my strength and my shield; my
heart trusts in him, and he helps me.

Living in a fallen world, brokenness is something we have all known. Sadly, an area where we often see much of this is in our relationships—parents and their children, husbands and wives, siblings and friends. Real relationships require vulnerability, and vulnerability leaves us open to potential hurt by those we love. And those are the wounds that hurt the most.

Our natural tendency is often to defend ourselves in such situations. While at times that may be an appropriate response, there are times when it is not. There are times when, no matter what you say, it will not be heard by the other person; it will not be received. And there are times when trying to do so does more harm than good. There may come a time when you can share the things that are on your heart, but sometimes people are not in a place to consider them at that moment. Praying for God's wisdom in those situations is vital.

I know how other people's responses, or lack thereof, can cause significant guilt and shame for the other person. Sometimes, even after we spend time in prayer and the Word, reminding ourselves of His love, grace, and forgiveness, we still struggle. Sometimes, the voice of shame and guilt can scream louder than the truth. It is then that we must press into Jesus with all our heart, soul, mind, and strength. We must continue to pray even if we feel like those prayers are bouncing off the ceiling. We must remain in God's Word, seeking it as if for treasure, letting it take root in our hearts that we may continually remember the truth. We must be careful to seek God alone for comfort and refuge so that we do not turn to things, or even some people, who would draw us away from God and cause more harm, leading us down a path of sin. This is how we fight against the lies that fill our hearts and minds and seek to take us down. This is how we put on the armor of God and stand with everything we've got.

We cannot control others or their responses. However, we are responsible for our own. Pray for wisdom, restoration, and victory over sin and the enemy, who seeks to destroy us and our relationships, leaving us feeling isolated, unlovable, and without value or worth, for the Bible warns us of our enemy, Satan. God's Word exhorts us to "be alert and of sober mind. Your enemy the devil prowls around like a roaring lion looking for someone to devour. Resist him, standing firm in the faith" (1 Pet. 5:8–9 [NIV]).

Last week, we read about God as a warrior in Zephaniah 3:17. I want to remind you that He is fighting for you always. Today, I would like to leave you with a line from one of my favorite worship songs: "Praise the Lord our mighty warrior, praise the Lord the glorious one. By Your hand we stand in victory. By Your name we overcome!"

38

Sensitivity to the Holy Spirit

Ephesians 5:19–20 (AMP)
Speak to one another in psalms and hymns and spiritual songs, [offering praise by] singing and making melody with your heart to the Lord; always giving thanks to God the Father for all things, in the name of our Lord Jesus Christ.

One day while I was driving, the song "The God Who Stays" by Matthew West came on the radio. I had been in recent conversations with a friend who was struggling with some incredibly painful things in her past, as well as regrets and fear. These things made it difficult to take hold of the truth of who she is in Christ and His unfailing love for her as His daughter. As I sat singing this song, thoughts of her filled my mind immediately and continued throughout the song as I listened carefully, taking in every word. Once I got home, I typed out part of the lyrics and emailed them to her with a personal message. In her response, she shared that those words came at the perfect time—that it was just what she needed. I knew in that moment that the Lord had used me to remind His beloved child of His unending love and faithfulness. I was filled with awe as I considered what a personal God we serve, one who loves us each individually and uniquely as a good Father does.

I hope my sharing this will encourage you to be sensitive to the Holy Spirit and His prompting. If you feel He is urging you to share a certain scripture, song, or passage with a particular person God has put on your heart, trust Him in that. I always pray in those situations, wanting to be as sure as possible that I'm doing the right thing, and I would encourage you to do the same. If you have a peace about it, step out in faith and follow His lead. You never know how God may use you and the words you share to bless someone, lift them up in their time of need, or remind them of the truth about who God is or who they are in Christ.

Just as I felt led to share a portion of that song with my friend, I also feel led to share those very same words with all of you.

> My shame can't separate
> My guilt can't separate
> My past can't separate
> I'm Yours forever
> My sin can't separate
> My scars can't separate
> My failures can't separate
> You're the God who stays
> ("The God Who Stays" by Matthew West [2020])

Read each line as many times as you need for those truths to set in. God truly is the one who stays—at all times and in all things. And He not only stays but also runs in our direction, especially in the times when those who should stay rather turn and walk away. Even in our sin and failures, our regrets and mistakes, God does not abandon us. When we turn to Him, whether in our pain and suffering, our guilt and shame, or our acknowledgement of sin and need to repent, He is already there waiting. At the first sign of our looking to Him, He runs to us, embraces us, forgives us, comforts us, and cleanses us. I hope you will take time this week to read the story of the Prodigal Son found in Luke 15:11–32. This is a story many of us know, but don't let familiarity with the passage keep you from taking time to sit with it, reading it slowly and intentionally, and asking the Lord to speak to you personally through it. God's Word is alive and active (Heb. 4:12) and speaks to us in different ways throughout the varied seasons of life. Don't miss what He wants to say to you.

39

Renewing Your Mind

Romans 12:2 (NKJV)
And do not be conformed to this world, but be transformed
by the renewing of your mind, that you may prove what
is that good and acceptable and perfect will of God.

Last week, I mentioned how God used a song and the prompting of His Spirit to bless and encourage a friend of mine through me. I trust that, if He has not already, God will use you to do the same for someone else—whether through His Word, worship music, or any myriad of things He may choose to use, for God's desire is that we "encourage each other and build each other up" (1 Thess. 5:11 [NLT]). But God, being the personal God that He is, also speaks to our hearts directly for our own benefit, giving a personal blessing and any encouragement we may need.

He does this, first and foremost, through His Word. The Bible is referred to as God's love letter to us, and I can understand why. From the first page to the last, it truly displays His extraordinary love for us. It tells us of the great lengths He went to, to reveal Himself and His love toward us and is filled with incredible promises to those who, in faith, believe and receive His gift of salvation. This is one of many reasons why memorizing scripture is so important. It reminds us who we are in Christ, what our eternal future will be like in His kingdom and presence, and how we experience God's blessing and favor not only then but also now as we seek to live our lives according to His will.

God can also use things, such as worship music, to speak to us and comfort our hearts because it is often rooted in the truths and promises of scripture. There's a song called "Good Grace" by Hillsong United, which many of you are probably familiar with. There was a time where every morning I would wake up and the very first thing in my head was the part of this song that says,

> Don't let your heart be troubled
> Don't fear no evil
> Fix your eyes on this one truth
> God is madly in love with you
> Take courage
> Hold on
> Be strong
> Remember where our help comes from
> ("Good Grace" by Hillsong United [2019])

From the moment I opened my eyes, I would just start singing it in my head. It was as if the Holy Spirit was saying, "These are the thoughts I want you to start your day with, not the negative ones, not the anxious and worry-filled ones, not the lies—but these words of hope, of love, and of help." It took me a few days to realize this had been happening first thing every morning, but, when I finally noticed, I was amazed.

I love God's Word, and I enjoy sitting with it, seeing His words of promise before my eyes, and highlighting certain passages that stand out to me. But I also love worship music and am thankful for those who have musical gifts and use their talents to honor God and help draw our hearts into a place of worship. There's something about setting the promises of God to a tune that helps plant the sweet and precious promises of scripture into our hearts and minds, bringing forth the fruit of praise to God from our hearts, mouths, and hands.

There are so many things that happen over the course of a day that can draw our attention away from Christ. But reading the Word daily and taking opportunities to listen to worship music, whether you're in the car or cleaning the house, exercising or relaxing, they keep our thoughts fixed on Him throughout the day. They keep us in conversation and fellowship with Him as we go about our everyday lives, which keeps Him at the center where He belongs. They also help us actively and continually renew our minds and redirect our thoughts when they start to stray. Therefore, I encourage you to take every opportunity to do both often! He will bring about change as you continually align yourself with His Word and set your affections on Him through worship and praise.

40

Worship

Psalm 100:2–3 (NLT)
Worship the LORD with gladness. Come before him, singing with joy. Acknowledge that the LORD is God! He made us, and we are his. We are his people, the sheep of his pasture.

Psalm 86:9–10 (AMP)
All nations whom You have made shall come and kneel down in worship before You, O LORD, and they shall glorify Your name. For You are great and do wondrous works! You alone are God.

John 4:24 (NKJV)
God is Spirit, and those who worship Him must worship in spirit and truth.

Last week, I touched on the topic of worship. This week I'd like to take it a little further. First, I would like to note that worship can be both an action and a state of being. We actively worship God through means such as prayer, praise, singing, and thanksgiving. Often, worshipping the Lord is a personal pursuit, one done in the quiet places of our homes, the solitude of our cars, or the privacy of our hearts. But it can also be done corporately, most often in church, where we come together as the body of Christ and, with one voice, sing praise and worship to our Father and Savior.

Worship can also be a state of being. Our everyday lives—our working and resting, our thoughts and our words, our tears and our laughter, our chaos and our peace, our busyness and stillness—all can be forms of worship if we allow them to be; if we are intentional about acknowledging God in all things, handing Him every moment in surrender, and offering a continual sacrifice of praise. In this way, our lives themselves become an endless harmony of worship.

The year 2020 dealt all of us some serious blows. The onset of COVID-19 literally turned our nation upside down in the blink of an eye and has forced us to change the way we live and interact with others. Everyone has faced challenges to one degree or another. Being unable to gather together as the body of Christ for a time undoubtedly impacted us all deeply. As the months went on and the church doors remained closed, I found myself truly missing corporate worship. I missed singing and praising God together as one body, with one voice, in the same Spirit—hearts overflowing with worship of our Father and Savior.

There's a song we sing at my church based on Psalm 46. I don't quite have words to explain how filled up and fired up this song makes me feel every time we sing it. The chorus says,

> Lord of Hosts, You're with us, with us in the fire
> With us as a shelter, with us in the storm
> You will lead us through the fiercest battle
> Oh, where else would we go, but with the Lord of
> Hosts?
> ("Psalm 46 [Lord of Hosts]" by Shane and Shane)

It reminds me that God is our Mighty Warrior (Zeph. 3:17). He is our strength and our shield (Ps. 28:7). He is ever present with each of us (Ps. 46:1). He is the conquering King who stands victorious over Satan, sin, and death (Rev. 17:4, 1:5–6, 19:13–16). His presence goes before us and is behind us (Ps. 139:5–6). Where else would we go, and to whom else would we turn but to Jesus Christ, our Savior? (John 6:68–69). The only unshakable foundation upon which we have to stand is Christ (Luke 6:46–49, 1 Cor. 3:10–11, Eph. 2:19–22, Isa. 28:16). He alone is the way, the truth, and the life (John 14:6).

My sisters, no matter what our personal circumstances are or what is going on in the world around us, let us live our lives with hearts that are full of worship to God. Let us all stand together in solidarity, in oneness of spirit, and proclaim the truth of these words as the battle cry of our hearts. Allow them to echo throughout your whole being even in the quietest, loneliest, and darkest of places. May they also be shouts of praise in times of victory, glorifying our Father and Savior!

41

Empathy

Galatians 6:2 (NIV)
Carry each other's burdens, and in this way
you will fulfill the law of Christ.

One day, a friend of mine and I were talking about compassion, empathy, and meeting others where they're at. We talked about the incredible gift they can be when shared, as well as the hurt that is often felt when they are not. She shared that if she ever got cancer, she would want to be under the care of a doctor who has had it himself or herself or knows someone personally who has had it. That doctor would not only be able to treat the disease but also have a sensitivity to all the other dynamics that are a part of going through that experience. As such circumstances would strengthen and fortify the doctor/patient relationship, she also believes that the suffering I've been through is what enables me to come alongside others to support and encourage them through difficult times. Sometime after that conversation, I read a quote that really struck me. It reads,

Jesus is God's wounded healer; through His wounds we are healed. Jesus' suffering and death brought joy and life. His humiliation brought glory; his rejection brought a community of love. As followers of Jesus we can also allow our wounds to bring healing to others." (Henry Nouwen)

I feel this beautifully conveys the heart behind what my friend was saying. When someone is deeply and intimately acquainted with suffering or grief, heartbreak or loneliness, pain or anguish, rejection or abandonment, or some other type of affliction or difficulty, one is often able to genuinely empathize and uniquely minister to others in a similar position. There is a level of compassion that can often scale the depths of someone else's darkness, without fear, because it is a familiar place to the person as well. There can be a level of understanding that brings a degree of healing to the heart, knowing that you are seen yet still loved—that you are understood but not judged. There is a sense of safety being in such a person's presence knowing that your heart will be handled with gentleness and care while in a fragile state.

For me, there are few things as precious as this level of connection and authenticity. How interesting it is that pain is what enables such a bond to be formed—that it is in darkness where we see the light of love and mercy shine most brightly. My friends, when we come to the place where we are able and willing to share our stories and show our wounds, God can use us as instruments of healing in the lives of others. I cannot think of a greater privilege.

I am eternally grateful for the people God has brought into my life at different times throughout what has been nearly a lifetime of suffering and pain that has touched every aspect of my life, physically, mentally, emotionally, and spiritually. Some of those relationships were for a season. Others have spanned many years and continue to be a blessing and a healing balm to this day. It is my heart's greatest desire to be a safe haven and a healing presence in the lives of others—showing the compassion, mercy, and grace of Jesus to the broken and the hurting. I hope you will join me in this pursuit.

42

Hope of Restoration

Psalm 42:11 (AMP)

Why are you in despair, O my soul? Why have you become restless and disquieted within me? Hope in God and wait expectantly for Him, for I shall yet praise Him, the help of my countenance and my God.

The older I get, the more I realize how little control we really have in so many areas of our lives. One area where it can be the most challenging and frustrating is in the realm of relationships, more specifically in regard to people's responses. There are times when people's reactions can be quite harsh. Even when there is no justification for such a response, it can be easy to internalize their words and actions. Then, suddenly, we start to feel the grip of shame overcomes us. Furthermore, feelings of fear and hopelessness for healing and restoration of the relationship can strengthen its hold.

First, I would like to say, any shame you feel under such circumstances is a liar. You are not responsible for other people's responses or reactions. You cannot control them. Each of us is responsible for our own words and actions to any given situation, and we are all accountable to God for them. However, fear of rejection or abandonment is real, and there is a possibility that this relationship that you value deeply may never be restored. This is one of many reasons why knowing the truths of God's word about who you are in Christ is so important—to know what He thinks of you and how He sees you as His child, His beloved. I hope you have many of these promises hidden in your heart already. It's also helpful to have a few key passages written down somewhere that is easily accessible. Therefore, if things turn out as you fear, and those feelings of rejection seek to supplant you, then you have the truths of God's word right there to read, recite to yourself, and refute the lies of the enemy and of shame, to stand firm and believe the promises of God, renewing your mind with them. Then every lie that comes to mind and every thought that contradicts what God's word says you will be able to silence, armed with His truths and promises to throw in the face of that lie.

While you prepare for the unwanted outcome, also pray and trust that God can bring about your desire to see that relationship restored. Believe that He is able to soften that persons' heart and bring about the healing that you seek. Unfortunately, we never know which way things will go. But I do know that God is good and that He is able to do exceedingly abundantly beyond all we could ask or imagine (Eph. 3:20). I know that He loves you both. I know that He loves family, for He created us to be in families, both earthly and spiritual ones. However, we don't always know how He is working behind the scenes or His purpose in allowing things that we can't understand. But I know He is faithful and He is able to make all things new.

I am praying for you right now—praying for the miraculous in every strained or severed relationship you may have because He is the God of the impossible. I think it gives Him joy to do the impossible on

43

Conviction

Psalm 103:11–18 (AMP)

For as the heavens are high above the earth, so great is His lovingkindness toward those who fear and worship Him [with awe-filled respect and deepest reverence]. As far as the east is from the west, so far has He removed our transgressions from us. Just as a father loves his children, so the LORD loves those who fear and worship Him [with awe-filled respect and deepest reverence]. For He knows our [mortal] frame; He remembers that we are [merely] dust. As for man, his days are like grass; Like a flower of the field, so he flourishes. For the wind passes over it and it is no more, and its place knows it no longer. But the lovingkindness of the LORD is from everlasting to everlasting on those who [reverently] fear Him, and His righteousness to children's children, to those who honor and keep His covenant, and remember to do His commandments [imprinting His word on their hearts].

Psalm 51:10 (ESV)
Create in me a clean heart, O God, and
renew a right spirit within me.

One day, while talking with a friend, she made a reference to God not being a slot machine. I recalled a few instances in the past where I needed to repent and ask forgiveness for treating God like He's my genie in a bottle. I can get into these modes where my prayer time goes a little something like this: "Can You do this? Can You do that? Would You mind doing this? Would please do that?" Then I hear His gentle whisper: "Is this all I am to you—someone to simply fulfill your wants and desires?" And my heart breaks with sadness and remorse.

Surely, God wants us to bring our petitions before Him—for ourselves, for our loved ones, and for the lost. In fact, His Word tells us, "Do not be anxious *or* worried about anything, but in everything [every circumstance and situation] by prayer and petition with thanksgiving, continue to make your [specific] requests known to God. And the peace of God [that peace which reassures the heart, that peace] which transcends all understanding, [that peace which] stands guard over your hearts and your minds in Christ Jesus [is yours]" (Phil. 4:6–7 [AMP]). Furthermore, He yearns to have a relationship with us. He desires to be known just as we long to be known. He wants our time in His Word and prayer to be a dialogue, not a one-way conversation. He is eager for us to seek Him at all times and in all things, great and small, and still ourselves long enough to hear His response.

When I take time to consider these things, I am astounded, humbled, and overwhelmed by the immensity of His love for me. Yet I can treat Him exactly the way that I do not want to be treated—as if I'm only worth someone's time if I'm doing something for them or they want something from me. It is heartbreaking to think that, at times, I have treated God in such a way, by no means intentionally, but I am guilty nonetheless. Yet He has been gracious both to bring this to my attention that I may repent, and to forgive me and restore to me the joy of His salvation (Ps. 51:12).

44

Godly Living

Proverbs 24:3–4 (AMP)
Through [skillful and godly] wisdom a house [a life, a home,
a family] is built, and by understanding it is established
[on a sound and good foundation], and by knowledge its
rooms are filled with all precious and pleasant riches.

First, this week's scripture tells us the fundamentals for living
a godly life: wisdom, understanding, and knowledge. When we
build our lives and our homes according to the wisdom of God's
Word, those who are not yet saved can't help but stand up and take
notice that there is something different about us. They see the light
of Christ in us and realize that there is something we have that they
are missing. It is one more way that we can be a witness to those who
are lost and broken around us, another opportunity to share the love
and grace of God and lead others to Christ. So let's pray that our
individual lives, marriages, and families not only bless those within
them but also set an example to those around us for God's glory and
for their salvation.

Second, we see the necessity of understanding. It's one thing to read God's Word and to memorize scripture, both of which are essential. In Psalm 119:11, the author states, "I have hidden Your word in my heart that I might not sin against You" (NIV). Not only does memorizing scripture keep us living according to it, but also I cannot count how many times the Holy Spirit has brought a certain verse to mind at just the right time—a particular promise of God to comfort me when I'm hurting, to reassure me when I'm doubting, and to strengthen me when I am weak and feeling utterly spent. But more important is having an accurate understanding of what it is saying. This is one of the many benefits of attending a Bible-centered church that teaches the Word in its entirety from a trusted pastor. Equally important is time spent in personal bible study as well as small group studies with fellow brothers and sisters in Christ. As members of the body of Christ, we are to glean from one another's insights and life experiences. We may all be at different places in our walk with the Lord, but everyone has something to contribute seeing how we are all filled with the same Spirit. The Bible tells us, "The one who gets wisdom loves life; the one who cherishes understanding will soon prosper" (Prov. 19:8 [NIV]).

This leads us to the last portion of our scripture this week: the importance of knowledge and the blessing it brings. We've discussed the centrality of God's Word and how it is the cornerstone upon which we build our lives. Next is the significance of an accurate understanding of His Word that gives us the secure foundation needed to grow. Last is the wisdom of the Holy Spirit needed to apply the knowledge gained to our everyday lives. All the understanding in the world is useless without the wisdom to walk it out. Therefore, in all these things, let us diligently and fervently seek the Holy Spirit to give us the wisdom to both understand and apply what we learn, that God's Word may indeed be a lamp to our feet and a light to our path (Ps. 119:105). As we do this, we will see fruit born from walking according to God's will for our lives and reap the precious and pleasant riches that He desires to give us.

45

Moving Mountains

Lamentations 3:22–23 (AMP)
It is because of the LORD's loving kindnesses
that we are not consumed, because His [tender]
compassions never fail. They are new every morning;
Great and beyond measure is Your faithfulness.

What I have for you today is a testimony of God's love, power, and faithfulness. While participating in a group bible study some time ago, I read this statement: "Keep in mind at all times that what God has entrusted to you might be for someone else." In that moment, I felt prompted to give an account of God's faithfulness and provision, an account of Him moving mountains on my behalf—that this part of my story was not only for me but also for the sake of someone else. Now, today, I believe He wants me to share it with you as well. I pray it speaks to your heart and strengthens your faith to believe Him for the impossible.

In 2011, less than two months before I was due to graduate from Philadelphia Biblical University, I received a letter stating that I owed thousands of dollars for tuition that had to be paid before graduation. I had financial aid throughout my studies that wasn't to be repaid until after graduation; therefore, I was quite taken aback. I tried to resolve the issue to no avail. I was told the money was due by graduation, or I could not walk. My heart sank. How could this be happening? I had worked harder for this Bible degree than I had for anything up until that point. My dad's plane tickets were already purchased. He was flying in from Missouri to see me graduate. I was upset and confused, literally crying out to God for His help. He responded, very clearly in my spirit, with one word: *fast*. I knew very little about fasting at that time but knew I needed to trust Him and obey. I assumed the issue would be resolved in a couple of days, but nothing. However, God continued to impress upon me the need to trust Him. Days and weeks went by. Letter after letter arrived with threats of being turned over to collections and the inability to participate in graduation if this was not reconciled. "Trust Me," He continued to say.

I recalled a passage in the Bible, 2 Kings 19:14–20, when Hezekiah received threatening letters from his adversaries. He spread the letters out before the Lord and prayed that God see their threats and that He deal with them personally. So I followed suit. I spread every letter out on my coffee table, got on my knees, and prayed that God would see their threats and be moved to act on my behalf. Later, it came time for my graduation rehearsal, yet nothing had been resolved. I prayed, not knowing what to do. "Go," He said. "Trust Me." So I went, full of anxiety that I'd be turned away at the door, but they let me in. I was part of the rehearsal, and no one questioned me. Then graduation day came, but still nothing. Again, He said, "Go, trust Me." That day, I had the privilege of walking across the stage to receive my diploma.

I spent the next few weeks in awe yet bewildered. The issue still had not been resolved. Even though I was able to participate in graduation, which was both a blessing and a miracle, I was still receiving letters about the debt. Then, one day out of the blue, I was approached by someone at church who handed me a check for over $6,000. She said it was from Jesus. She originally had other plans for this money, but they were thwarted. Then she heard about my situation and felt God clearly call her to give the money to me. She shared that she had a full ride for her college degree and believed God was calling her to pay it forward.

I truly do not have words to describe this experience. Awe and amazement still fill me with tears as I recall God's love, Him working to stretch and strengthen my faith, and His miraculous provision on my behalf. I believe what He wants to say to you today is "Trust Me. With reckless abandon, trust Me. In every moment of fear, doubt, and confusion, trust Me." Whatever Mountain, whatever "impossible" stands before you, it is no match for our God. He has storehouses of treasures in the heavens that He is able to pour out upon you—blessing upon blessing until it overflows. Lift your hands in faith and surrender to the Lord, affirming this truth: "Ah, LORD God! Behold, You have made the heavens and the earth by Your great power and outstretched arm. There is nothing too hard for You" (Jer. 32:17, [NKJV]).

46

Accountability

Romans 5:8 (NIV)
But God demonstrates His own love for us in this:
While we were still sinners, Christ died for us.

As a result of our fallen nature, selfishness and self-centeredness are very much a part of the human condition. Not one of us is exempt. Our sinful nature is always looking for opportunities to gratify itself, bucking against the truths and instructions of scripture, and luring us into a lifestyle that brings pain and destruction—a life that has enmity toward God and a love for self and for pleasure. The Bible tells us, "The heart is deceitful above all things and it is extremely sick. Who can understand it fully and know its secret motives?" (Jer. 17:9 [AMP]). Therefore, we are not to "follow our heart" as the world tells us to do. We are to lead our hearts according to what we know is right. Throughout the Bible, we see clearly that love is a choice. Yes, it can also be a feeling, and a lovely feeling at that! But we all know that feelings come and go. They are dependent upon our mood, circumstances, desires, and the like. Therefore, ultimately, love is a choice. Let us determine, here and now, to choose it every day.

We cannot control the actions and choices of others. However, as far as we're concerned, let's make sure that we are accountable to God for the things we say and do. May we be ever more committed to abiding by His Word and His charge to love one another and forgive one another, to fight for one another and protect one another, to love sacrificially just as Jesus has loved and continues to love us. But remember: we cannot do this in our own strength. God is love, and He is the source of love. We must remain connected to the Vine— that is, Jesus—if we are to bear the fruit of Christ's love in our lives, for without Him, we can do nothing (John 15:5).

47

Priorities

Psalm 107:1 (AMP)
O give thanks to the LORD, for He is good; For His
compassion and lovingkindness endure forever!

A friend of mine once shared a longstanding and deeply rooted desire for her family's approval—a desire that sadly has been unmet throughout her life no matter the effort put forth. It has caused feelings of intense pain and wounding that have spanned many years. I shared with her that I can understand in some ways. For me, however, it is not so much approval as it is a yearning to be accepted—to belong. I desire to be loved for who I am—to be wanted.

I don't think anyone's desire to have their family's support and approval, or one's desire to be wanted and accepted is bad in and of itself. I believe God created us to be in loving relationships where there is both acceptance and a sense of belonging—relationships where you encourage one another and reaffirm your love and commitment to those people regularly. But, sadly, God's design for family, marriage, and many other things has been marred by sin.

Often, it doesn't look anything like God's original design. Although that doesn't change the desire within us for those things that we were created for.

However, the place and priority we give that desire in our lives can be a problem. When that longing becomes greater than our longing for God, greater than a desire for His love, His approval, His fellowship, it becomes detrimental to our well-being, physically, mentally, emotionally, and spiritually, because He was always meant to be first in our lives. We are unable to truly live, know peace, and bear fruit in our lives when we aren't connected to the Vine (John 15:1–5), when God is not the source from which we draw for all of our needs, when He isn't the one and only source of true fulfillment and satisfaction in our hearts.

Maybe some of you share this struggle, whether it be the same feelings mentioned above or any multitude of others. Maybe you've been feeling the Lord tugging at your heart, gently but firmly, showing you that you have left your first love (Rev. 2:4). If that is you today, there is good news. You're recognizing that this has been true for you, and that is the first step. You're becoming aware that "humankind" has had a greater place in your heart than God. You are by no means the only one! I believe it is true for each one of us at different times throughout our lives. What is important is that you acknowledge it when the Holy Spirit reveals it to you and respond. "Consider how far you have fallen! Repent and do the things you did at first" (Rev. 2:5 [NIV]). Be intentional about making the changes needed to reorganize and prioritize the people and things in your life where God is first, where He is at the center. Then the rest will start to fall into place.

The best news? God is gracious to forgive us. He knows we get things wrong time and again, and He is always faithful to show us when we've gotten off track. He waits with anticipation for us to come to Him, admit our sin, and seek His forgiveness so that He can cleanse us from all our unrighteousness and realign our hearts with His. "For as high as the heavens are above the earth, so great is His love for those who fear Him; as far as the east is from the west, so far has he removed our transgressions from us. As a father has compassion on his children, so the LORD has compassion on those who fear Him; for He knows how we are formed, He remembers that we are dust" (Ps. 103:11–14 [NIV]).

48

Thanksgiving

2 Corinthians 4:6 (NIV)
For God, who said, "Let light shine out of darkness," made
his light shine in our hearts to give us the light of the
knowledge of God's glory displayed in the face of Christ.

Thanksgiving as a lifestyle is something the Lord has been
speaking to me about personally. He has been showing me how I
can become so bogged down by the difficulties in life that I don't
always recognize the many things I have to be thankful for. I don't
always see the blessings that are mingled in with the suffering. Truly,
it is gratitude and thankfulness to God that lift us out of the pit and
transform our thinking no matter the circumstances we may find
ourselves in. As His Word says, we were created to "shine as lights
in the world" (Phil. 2:15 [NKJV]). So often I have prayed, asking
Jesus to cause His light and presence to shine forth from me—that
He would help me to reflect His character; that when others look
at me, they would see Him. He has been teaching me that it is
thankfulness and praise to Him that ignite us from the inside out.
They enable us to shine as He intended and give Him the glory He
so rightly deserves.

Help us, Lord, not to be bogged down by the weight we each carry but to continually cast our cares and our burdens on You—that your light in us would not be dimmed. May the thankfulness in our hearts be multiplied one hundredfold. May Your light shine forth from our lives, blazing in radiance, that we may be better witnesses for You. In Jesus's name, I pray. Amen.

49

Hope amid Suffering

Luke 22:42 (NKJV)
Father, if it is Your will, take this cup away from Me;
nevertheless not My will, but Yours, be done.

Once, I found myself confronted by a bible study question that asked if I have been stripped of my own personal agenda. In all honesty, for years, I've tried to have no agenda—no specific dreams or goals to achieve. Truly, my prayer has been "Not my will, but Yours be done." Yet, over a seven-year period, God chose to strip me of almost everything else. I had lost my career and my ability to earn a personal income. My health and mobility steadily declined. I was stripped of physical strength and stamina that made even the simplest days feel like I was trudging up a mountain. He allowed me to suffer physical and emotional pain that stole my breath away and isolated me from the world that continued to move around me. I have never felt more alone, more vulnerable, or more weak. But His Word says that it is in our weakness that He is most strong (2 Cor. 12:10).

Years ago, I prayed for some time that I would "know Him and the power of His resurrection, the fellowship of His sufferings, being conformed to His death" (Phil. 3:10 [NKJV]). It appears He was pleased to answer that prayer. He has poured out on me the fellowship of His sufferings and has indeed been conforming me to His death. Therefore, if He has been faithful to answer those two parts of the prayer, then, surely, He will be faithful to show me the power of His resurrection in my life as well. His transforming, healing, and redemptive power is more than able to restore the years the locusts have eaten (Joel 2:25).

As I wait, Lord, help me to remember continually that "I can do all things [which He has called me to do] through Him who strengthens and empowers me [to fulfill His purpose—I am self-sufficient in Christ's sufficiency; I am ready for anything and equal to anything through Him who infuses me with inner strength and confident peace.]" (Phil. 4:13 [AMP]). Let my story and Your story of redemption continue to be intertwined that a new story may unfold—one that reveals Your purpose and brings fulfillment of Your will in and through my life. In Jesus's name, I pray. Amen.

50

Drought

Jeremiah 17:7–8 (NIV)
Blessed is the one who trusts in the LORD, whose confidence is in Him. They will be like a tree planted by the water that sends out its roots by the stream. It does not fear when heat comes; its leaves are always green. It has no worries in a year of drought and never fails to bear fruit.

All of us experience seasons of drought in our lives. The lack that we experience can be material, relational, or spiritual, to name a few. During these times of drought, we are often faced with temptation. Maybe it's to obtain finances in an illegitimate way or to determine that you're going to get what you want regardless of whether you have the means, only to find yourself buried under credit card debt. Maybe it's temptation to seek out an inappropriate relationship with someone you feel will give you the attention and affection that you long for in hopes to rid yourself of the emptiness you feel. Or you turn to food in attempts to fill yourself with the comfort your heart and body crave. Maybe it's the temptation to doubt God's goodness, faithfulness, and promises in times of difficulty or spiritual dryness when your prayers feel like they're falling on deaf ears or repeatedly hitting the ceiling. You pour out your heart continually only to hear nothing but silence.

There is no question whether drought will come but when, as we see in our verse for this week. But what we also see is that when we trust, hope, and place our full confidence in the Lord during such times, He brings forth blessing. When we resist the temptations that seek to undo us and turn to Him to provide a way out that we may endure (1 Cor. 10:13), He enables us to bear fruit even in the most barren seasons of life. Our confidence in Him strengthens our faith as we dig deep; our roots grow longer and stronger as we draw from the rivers of living water—that is, His Spirit. Jesus Himself beckons, "If anyone is thirsty, let him come to me and drink! He who believes in Me [who adheres to, trusts in, and relies on Me], as the Scripture has said, 'From his innermost being will flow continually rivers of water'" (John 7:37–38 [AMP]). This is how our fears and doubts are quenched in times of drought. Instead of withering from the oppressive heat of our circumstances, we can thrive—filled with life-giving water to share with others.

Let me just say this has been a hard lesson to learn—one that I am still working through. I have been in seemingly endless seasons of drought. However, it is the place where God has chosen to slowly but surely bring healing to my heart and life. I have come to be thankful for this process He has been taking me through. While it has been difficult, painful, and lonely, Jesus has revealed Himself to me in incredibly personal ways. He has spoken gently to my heart. He has poured out His grace on me and my fears, doubts, and anxieties. He has continually assured me of His unfailing love for me. I have come to know personally His tenderness, His provision, and His promise to never leave me or forsake me. If it were not for such suffering, I don't know if I would have had the privilege of the intimate experiences with the Lord over the years. I wouldn't trade them for anything.

Whatever drought you may find yourself in presently or in the future, remember this promise: "You shall eat in plenty and be satisfied, and praise the name of the LORD your God, who has dealt wondrously with you; And My people shall never be put to shame … I am the LORD your God and there is no other. My people shall never be put to shame" (Joel 2:26–27 [NKJV]).

51

Blessed Assurance

Isaiah 9:6 (NIV)

For to us a Child is born, to us a Son is given, and
the government will be on His shoulders. And
He will be called Wonderful Counselor, Mighty
God, Everlasting Father, Prince of Peace.

As followers of Christ, may we continually bring to remembrance and celebrate the day God's rescue plan for us became flesh over two thousand years ago. He will come again, in all His glory, to utterly destroy evil forever. We will spend eternity together in His kingdom, where there will be no more crying, pain, suffering, or death (Rev. 21:4). Because of Jesus, our hope will become our reality! Our faith will become our sight! We will live forever where there is only light continually.

Thank you, Jesus, for Your willingness to lay Your glory aside and come to us in human flesh, born as a baby, as one who lived and suffered as we do and who understands our weaknesses, so that you could be our High Priest, filled with compassion and understanding (Heb. 4:16).

We praise you God for the unimaginable gift of Your only Son so that we could be saved, healed, restored, and redeemed! You are worthy of all our praise! I pray You lift any weight of heaviness in our hearts today and, instead, fill them with overflowing glory and praise to You for all that You have done and will continue to do! In Jesus's great and precious name, I pray. Amen!

52

Firm Foundation

Romans 15:13 (AMP)
May the God of hope fill you with all joy and peace in
believing [through the experience of your faith] that by
the power of the Holy Spirit you will abound in hope
and overflow with confidence in His promises.

With each new year that lies before us, we are faced with new
measures of both uncertainty and possibility, trials and opportunity.
Therefore, I want to encourage you with the hope we have in Jesus.
Our hope in Christ is not fleeting like the things of the world; it is
not here today and gone tomorrow, like the flowers of the fields (1 Pet.
1:24). Hebrews 6:19 assures us, "This hope we have as an anchor of the
soul, [is] both sure and steadfast" (NKJV). Another translation states,
it is both "strong and trustworthy" (NLT). And yet another adds,
"It cannot slip and it cannot break down under whatever pressure
bears upon it—a safe and steadfast hope" (AMP). Furthermore, God
promises repeatedly that our hope in Him will never put us to shame
(1 Pet. 2:6, Rom. 10:11, Isa. 54:4, Joel 2:26).

You are His beloved. Whatever this next year brings, nothing is going to change that. No failure, sin, doubt, or fear; no economic or political paradigm shift; no pandemic, present or future. You are a daughter of the Most High God, and in Him you are secure, come what may for we have this promise: "The LORD will fulfill His purpose for me; Your steadfast love, O LORD, endures forever" (Ps. 138:8 [ESV]).

Our hope in Christ is the only hope that cannot be shaken. Our salvation in Christ is the only assurance we have for this life and the next. "The Spirit Himself bear[ing] witness with our spirit that we are children of God, and if children, then heirs—heirs of God and joint heirs with Christ" (Rom. 8:16–17 [NKJV]). Therefore, let us be careful not to place our hope in government or social change but in Christ alone. Everything else will fail or fall short. Christ alone can save. Christ alone redeems and restores. He is the only one who never fails.

This coming year, let us fix our eyes on Him and commit our lives to Him like never before. Let us make our daily prayer that of Psalm 139:23–24: "Search me, God, and know my heart; test me and know my anxious thoughts. See if there is an offensive way in me, and lead me in the way everlasting" (NIV). Let us be intentional that our talk is our walk—that we are living out daily the faith and hope in Christ that we claim. Let us be the hands and feet of Jesus that our light may shine before others—that they may see our good works and glorify the Father (Matt. 5:16). And may we "always be prepared to give an answer to everyone who asks [us] to give the reason for the hope that [we] have with gentleness and respect" (1 Pet. 3:15 [NIV]).

Last, I would like to leave you with a few verses from one of my favorite worship songs based on one of our scriptures this week, Hebrews 6:19. I pray it will fill you with the utmost hope, comfort, and peace.

This anchor for my soul, this everlasting hope
Your grace on which I stand
It's where my life begins, my future held within
Your grace on which I stand
Oh, this grace on which I stand
It will hold me to the end, never failing
Oh, praise the One who rescued me
Jesus, You will ever be my salvation

EPILOGUE

Well, my friends, we have reached the end of the road. Thank you for journeying along with me through this past year of weekly devotions. When it became clear that the Lord was giving me this writing assignment, I was surprised, scared, excited, nervous, and overwhelmed by the privilege to speak into the hearts and lives of women—my fellow sisters in Christ. I am honored to have had the opportunity to encourage you each week, to share the compassion of Christ, to exhort you to seek the Lord through prayer and His Word, and to remind you of His unwavering faithfulness and unfailing love.

While I believe wholeheartedly that God's intent for these devotions was to encourage and comfort all of you, the truth is God used this time to speak deeply to my own heart as well. This process has stretched me, blessed me, convicted me, challenged me, and strengthened me. Truly, His faithfulness knows no bounds. His love knows no limit. His forgiveness never runs dry. He is relentless in His pursuit to rid us of the things that are not of Him, to free us from the sins that so easily entangle us, and to continually mold and shape us into the image of His Son.

God is faithful to His Word and His promises. There is no power like that of the Almighty. "With God all things are possible" (Matt. 19:26). This truth is one I hope you will take into the new year with you. Whatever your most desperate prayer, whatever your deepest longing, whatever "impossible" stands before you, trust that He is able even when you are not, for He has made the heavens and the earth by His great power and outstretched arm. There is nothing too hard for Him (Jer. 32:17). He "is able to [carry out His purpose and] do superabundantly more than all that we dare ask or think [infinitely beyond our greatest prayers, hopes, or dreams], according to His power that is at work within us" (Eph. 3:20).

Printed in the United States
by Baker & Taylor Publisher Services